"If you experience real life realities and st
but predictable spiritual platitudes are rii
is a resource that brings honesty and genuine hope. j___
depths of dependence himself, and shares candidly and practically to guide
you to experiencing the One worthy of all of our trust."

David Robbins
President & CEO, FamilyLife

"If you are longing for a faith that would be described as strongly rooted,
you have found the right book. As you read, you will clearly see why I feel so
honored to not merely have Jeff as my successor but also now as my pastor-
teacher. His life, leadership, and pastoring are all founded on what he will
describe to you in this book—'a lifestyle of radical dependence.' Enjoy and be
blessed by this excellent read."

Randy Pope
Founding pastor, Perimeter Church
Founder and president of Life on Life Ministries

"When the job is bigger than you are, the temptation is always to fake it until
you make it—or it breaks you. Pastor Jeff Norris's transparent acknowledgment
of panic when faced with pastoral challenges larger than he, will resonate
with anyone trying to do the job of living as God requires. But when Pastor
Jeff's panic led to a path of dependence on his Savior's grace, rather than
a performance treadmill, the gospel took deeper root in his life and his
congregation's. The result is the message of this book that is a delight to read,
not only because it rings true with the gospel but also rings true with the man
who is rooted in grace for his (and his people's) growth in Christ."

Bryan Chapell
Stated clerk, Presbyterian Church in America

"My friend Jeff Norris has given us a gift! As you see from the title, this
wonderful book is a clear, compelling call to a lifestyle of radical dependence
on the Lord. Thanks, Jeff, for underscoring that this kind of dependence should
be a reality in the life of every follower of Christ. I love the practical, engaging
way that Jeff invites us to make the commitment and embrace the journey.
This valuable resource will not only enrich your walk with Christ, but you will
want to place it in the hands of others."

Dr. Crawford W. Loritts, Jr.
Author, speaker, radio host
Founder and president of Beyond Our Generation

"Given the storms that rage in our culture today, Christians not rooted in a lifestyle of radical dependence will be especially exposed. Jeff Norris is a reliable guide to where shelter can be found and the practices of Christians who stand strong in any climate."

Collin Hansen
VP and editor in chief of The Gospel Coalition
Host of the *Gospelbound* podcast

"What a liberating book! Jeff Norris has given us an honest and wonderful tonic for the anxious, the spiritually bored, the legalistic, and the proud. For your health, peace, and joy: take and read!"

Rev. Dr. Michael Reeves
President and professor of theology
Union School of Theology

"I've had the pleasure of knowing Jeff for many years as lead teacher at Perimeter Church and also as a mentor and leader of a small group for the last two. One thing that is consistent each week in our group is the belief that we need God in every aspect of our lives. This book will outline the seven major roots of radical dependence. So whether you're a believer, or seeking answers about the Messiah, Jeff will equip you to find the truth and build an intimate relationship with the One True King. I hope you enjoy this book as much as I have, and more importantly, that it gets you rooted in Scripture and Truth."

Jeff Francoeur
Lead television analyst for Atlanta Braves games
Former outfielder for the Atlanta Braves

"I've had the privilege of working alongside Jeff for many years now, and what he writes in this book exemplifies the dependence on Jesus that he lives out both personally and as our head pastor. I recommend this book to anyone who is seeking to understand what true faith should look like in the daily life of a believer. *Rooted* calls out the lie that followers of Christ must be anything more than utterly dependent on Jesus."

Laura Story
Grammy Award-winning artist and author

ROOTED

A LIFESTYLE OF **RADICAL DEPENDENCE**

JEFF NORRIS

Rooted: A Lifestyle of Radical Dependence

Copyright © 2021 by Jeff D. Norris

Perimeter Church
9500 Medlock Bridge Road
Johns Creek, GA 30097
perimeter.org

ISBN 13-digit: 978-1-947106-11-6

Library of Congress Control Number: 2021920599

Cover Design: John Morris
Layout: Zach Wagoner
Printing: New London
Printed in the United States of America

ACKNOWLEDGMENTS

To Rachel, Samuel, Ellie Kate, Abigail, and Annie: My wife, my children, my world. You all get to see every side of me, and you love me the same. Thank you for being a constant reflection of the love and grace of our God in your daily lives. I love you!

To Lanny and Donna Norris: You raised me to love Jesus—words could never express my gratitude.

To Dexter and Martha Wood: You raised Rachel to love Jesus—words could never express my gratitude.

To Jennifer, Buddy, Ryan, and Erin: Thank you for being the awesome family that you are!

To Laura Story: You believed in me and pushed me to write this book long before I believed in myself. Even more, you have spent countless hours reading it, offering advice, promoting, networking, and championing me and this book. I can't thank you enough!

To Jamey Short: You and Laura are a powerfully persuasive duo! Thanks for originating the idea and pushing me to see it through.

To Leigh McElroy: Your writing and editing abilities are second to none! Thank you for the time you invested in this book to make it a reality.

To Bill Wood and Philip Hoffman: For the many hours you spent reading, researching, and editing my many mistakes!

To Randy Pope, Bill Wood, Gordon Moore, and Dan Case: A young leader and pastor couldn't ask for a better set of mentors and models of godly leadership and radical dependence.

To Eric Ryan, Stacey Earnest, and Chip Sweney: Many pastors can only dream of working with and alongside an executive leadership team as gifted and godly as you. I'm truly blessed to labor for the kingdom of God in the trenches with you!

To John Morris and Zach Wagoner: Your creative minds amaze me along with your incredible ability to take ideas and make them reality!

To Jackie Lucas: The world's best ministry associate, assistant, and friend! You bring order to my chaotic schedule and life, and your wisdom and insight is truly invaluable.

To the Perimeter Church family: It is a privilege beyond measure to serve as your pastor. You have faithfully loved and encouraged me. Thank you! I watch in amazement as the Lord powerfully brings the transformative work of his kingdom to bear through you in greater Atlanta and throughout the world!

CONTENTS

INTRODUCTION

ROOTED: A LIFESTYLE OF RADICAL DEPENDENCE

IN THE FALL OF 2018, RANDY POPE, PERIMETER CHURCH'S FOUNDING PASTOR, TOLD ME THAT HE AND THE LEADERSHIP OF THE CHURCH WERE LOOKING TO ME AS HIS SUCCESSOR. AFTER I HAD A SLIGHT PANIC ATTACK AND PICKED MY JAW OFF THE FLOOR, I HAD ONE OVERWHELMING THOUGHT: "THIS WILL TAKE A LEVEL OF DEPENDENCE UPON GOD THAT I'M NOT SURE I'VE EVER KNOWN."

At the time that Randy had spoken to me about this, it had been more than forty years since he had planted Perimeter Church. Over those forty years, the Lord had used him to grow the church significantly in attendance, membership, spiritual depth, and kingdom impact. Furthermore, Randy had been a long-time mentor to me. My walk with Jesus was in large part because of God's work in my life through Randy. "Who am I," I thought, "to follow in his footsteps?!" I immediately sensed that an endeavor like this would require something much more than casual dependence or an every-now-and-then dependence. I felt then, and continue to feel today, my own desperate need for a lifestyle of radical dependence.

The premise of this book is that this type of dependence upon the Lord—a radical dependence—is not just for soon-to-be senior pastors who are overwhelmed by the calling God has placed on them, but it's a dependence that is to be present and displayed in every follower of Christ on a daily basis. Jesus taught his disciples, *"From everyone who has been given much, much will be required; and to whom they entrusted much, of him they will ask all the more"* (Luke 12:48 NASB). We have all been given much in Christ. We have all been entrusted with much as stewards of his kingdom. I am convinced that all Christ followers, whether we are new to the faith or have followed him for decades, must be rooted in radical dependence upon God to do what only he can do in and through us, for his glory.

Rooted: A Lifestyle of Radical Dependence is adapted from the first sermon series I preached as Perimeter Church's senior pastor in the fall of 2019. In this book, we'll explore seven "roots" of radical dependence, all of which are anchored in the Word of God. Isaiah 61:3 says, *"that they may be called oaks of righteousness, the planting of the* LORD, *that he may be glorified."* As we seek to be oaks of righteousness who are planted by the Lord for his glory, we need to consider the types of biblical roots, if you will, that nourish and support an "oak of righteousness."

Each year we are faced with challenges that seem to be insurmountable, but in reality, they reveal our need to be deeply rooted. But what are we to be rooted in as followers of Christ? God's Word calls us to be people who are rooted in prayer, repentance, self-denial and sacrifice, obedience, discipleship, forgiveness and generosity, and thanksgiving. My prayer is that in these pages you will either discover for the first time or be reminded in a fresh way of the joy and flourishing that accompanies a life that is rooted in radical dependence.

Before we jump in, there's an important question I want you to consider: Are there recurring circumstances in your life that cause you to remember how not in control you are and how dependence upon yourself just won't cut it? There are two such recurring circumstances in my life: flying and preaching. I've traveled a lot over the years and continue to do so. My travels have taken me all over the continental United States and throughout the world. Yet, no matter how many times I fly in an airplane, I just can't get comfortable with the idea of rocketing through the air at 35,000 feet in a several hundred-ton hunk of metal! But the issue really isn't flying, it's what flying exposes about my heart, which is that I don't like realizing anew that I'm not in control. And when I keenly sense that I'm not in control, I freshly realize how completely dependent on something or someone else I am for my well-being.

Preaching is similar. Although I feel a bit more in control in the sense that I'm the one speaking, I know all too well that my words carry no power unless the Lord quickens and awakens the hearts of those listening to receive his Word.

I have often said that I long for my prayer life and my expression of dependence upon the Lord to be as radical every day of my life as it is when I'm about to board a plane or step on a stage to preach! That's what I'm aiming for in this book—to help you and me be rooted in radical dependence upon God, every single day of our lives, not just in special situations or circumstances. This is the life he has called us to—to embark on a faith journey with him that forces us into a lifestyle of radical dependence!

CHAPTER 1

WHAT DOES IT MEAN TO BE ROOTED?

THAT YOU, BEING ROOTED AND GROUNDED IN LOVE, MAY HAVE STRENGTH TO COMPREHEND WITH ALL THE SAINTS WHAT IS THE BREADTH AND LENGTH AND HEIGHT AND DEPTH, AND TO KNOW THE LOVE OF CHRIST THAT SURPASSES KNOWLEDGE, THAT YOU MAY BE FILLED WITH ALL THE FULLNESS OF GOD.

(EPHESIANS 3:17B-19)

I have never claimed to have a green thumb. Sometimes the plants I tend grow, and sometimes they don't. Sometimes I know why they grow, and sometimes I don't. On one occasion, a particular bush in our backyard suffered a pretty obvious failure to thrive. It was supposed to have lots of rich, green foliage, strong stems and lush, colorful blooms. But it didn't. Instead, it had faded to a sick shade of yellow. Its stems were thin and weak, and the blooms were almost non-existent.

I assumed I was dealing with a water problem. I don't know much about gardening, but I know plants require water. So, I watered it. A lot. In hindsight I probably gave it too much water, but nothing really changed. If anything, the plant became even more frail. Finally, in frustration I decided it was time to rip the uncooperative bush out of the ground and start over with a brand new one from the nursery.

Despite its pitiful condition, the bush was large and I assumed its roots were deep. So, I stooped down, encircled its base with both hands, and gave a huge tug to yank it from the ground. In seconds I found myself on my back, holding on to a bush with hardly any roots at all. I could have pulled it from the ground with one hand! My plant didn't need more water; all the water in Georgia wouldn't

---

have helped it. It needed support and nutrients from the kind of solid root system it was obviously lacking.

ROOTED TO FLOURISH

The Bible often uses botanical imagery to illustrate the need for God's people to be rooted in order to flourish. Paul prayed for his newly believing friends in the church at Ephesus, *"That you, being rooted and grounded in love, may have strength to comprehend with all the saints what is the breadth and length and height and depth, and to know the love of Christ that surpasses knowledge, that you may be filled with all the fullness of God"* (Ephesians 3:17b–19).

The apostle knew that God's people must be deeply rooted in Christ and his love in order to grow and flourish in a healthy and God-glorifying way. God desires for his people to exist in a vibrant love relationship with him, where their roots of dependence run deep and their faith blooms. Rooted, they can begin to experience the fullness of his presence and power in their lives.

In the two thousand years since Paul penned these words, nothing has changed. If we want to flourish as God's people, individually and corporately, we must be deeply rooted people: radically dependent on God to do what only he can do, in and through us. The challenge is this: we live in a world that applauds self-reliance, self-sufficiency, and self-righteousness. Many of us, even in the church, have bought into the deception that we are "self-made"—this is especially true for those of us who find ourselves living in the individualistic societies of the western culture. Let me say, being able to live one's life independently and self-reliant is not in and of itself bad, provided we recognize that we have been made by our Creator to look to him for our being, purpose, and self-reliance. We must be rooted in the rich soil of a vibrant relationship with the Father, and that alone will result in our flourishing. We sense deep within us that flourishing is out there to be discovered. We crave it! However, when we make idols out of our abilities, our independence, or our accomplishments we will find ourselves disillusioned and longing for more. (More on this in chapter 3!)

BEHAVIOR MODIFICATION VS. SPIRITUAL TRANSFORMATION

For many, there is a misunderstanding of the essence of Christianity. In a genuine effort to please God, we imagine that what he most wants from us is good behavior and right choices. What we soon discover, however, is that this leads not to joy and flourishing but to perpetual exhaustion on the hamster wheel of behavior modification. The truth is, there is nothing I can self-manage, manipulate, or achieve to earn the approval of God. What I *can* do is die to myself and my endless efforts of behavior modification and simply present myself to God, asking him to do a transforming work in me that only he can do through Christ. Apart from him, I really can do nothing (John 15:5)!

I didn't begin to truly understand this until I was a college sophomore (the year of the "wise fool"). Even though my parents taught me the gospel of grace, for a long time I defaulted to a version of Christianity that centered around my ability to modify my behavior rather than God's ability to transform my heart. I think some of this was due to the cultural context I grew up in. In my small town, deep South context, to be a "good Christian boy" meant to be polite, respectful, and involved in church. Most importantly, it meant avoiding the "big three don'ts": Don't get drunk or do drugs. Don't have sex. Don't cuss. Now, you have to understand … I'm a chronic people-pleaser. I *love* when people think well of me. So, when you mix a behavioral-centered Christianity with a people-pleasing temperament, you end up with a lethal cocktail of pride-fueled behavior modification that will ultimately drive you farther away from Christ than toward him.

It was during my freshman year at the University of Alabama where God exposed the shallowness of what I thought were deep spiritual roots. I joined a fraternity and quickly learned that my good behavior and right choices didn't win the approval and affirmation of my new fraternity brothers like it had at home.

One evening at the fraternity house stands out in my memory. My fellow pledges and I were standing along the wall in the dining room, waiting to serve the brothers' dinner. One of the upperclassmen called me over and pointed to the chair next to him. When I sat down, he said, "Why are you the way you are? You don't get drunk. You don't have sex. You don't cuss. You don't have fun. Why are you such a Goody Two-shoes?"

I didn't know what to say. So, I said the only thing I knew to say … "Umm, because I'm a Christian."

He said, "What does that have to do with anything?" (But in much more colorful language.) "Why is it that Christians can't have any fun?"

Again, I didn't know what to say. I was at a loss as to *why* my beliefs should impact the way I live. Up until that moment, being a good Christian had always gotten me what I most desired in life: recognition, respect, a good reputation, and accolades. Now, in that moment, it was occurring to me in a new way that if I wanted the approval of this guy—and the rest of my new fraternity brothers—something would have to change.

So, for the rest of that year, I conformed my life to theirs. My former commitment to expected and accepted behavior failed me when real pressure came. There were no roots to sustain the faith I proclaimed. The Christian beliefs that had temporarily affected my behavior for the good had somehow left my heart unchanged. My roots were shallow, and they were being exposed as the waters of the culture around me eroded away my previous notions of Christianity.

Maybe you've had a similar experience. Many of us, either in the past or even now, have misunderstood Christianity to be primarily about rooting ourselves in the religious routines of trying harder, being better, and doing good. As a result, we've suffered for relying on this kind of "get it together-ism" while missing the deeper rooted work of transformation God wants to do in our hearts.

God's desire isn't that we would give ourselves to various self-improvement projects that are wrapped in spirituality or religion. His desire is that we would simply give ourselves to him by trusting wholly and completely in the finished work of Christ on our behalf. When we are rooted in Jesus, connected to him, and depending upon him for life and power, we begin to see and experience his transforming glory in our lives.

QUESTIONS FOR REFLECTION

1. As we consider the example of a garden, why is being rooted a necessary requirement for flourishing?

2. Do you agree with the cultural belief of being "self-made"? How has your culture or even your upbringing encouraged this individualistic idea?

3. In your own words describe the difference in behavior modification and spiritual transformation. Is this type of distinction a new concept for you?

4. Describe a challenge in your life that seemed insurmountable. How has it brought you to a place of deeper dependence on God?

5. What changes need to be made to intentionally sink your roots deeper in Jesus and less in your own self-reliance?

CHAPTER 2

ROOTED IN
RADICAL
VERTICAL
DEPENDENCE

I'VE ALREADY TOLD YOU HOW BEING CONSIDERED AS RANDY POPE'S SUCCESSOR BROUGHT MY NEED FOR RADICAL DEPENDENCE ON THE LORD INTO LASER-SHARP FOCUS. BELIEVE ME, MY AWARENESS OF MY OWN WEAKNESSES AND INSECURITIES SKYROCKETED WHEN THAT POTENTIAL ROLE BEGAN TO BECOME A REALITY. I KNEW BEYOND A SHADOW OF DOUBT THAT ONLY GOD COULD EQUIP AND SUSTAIN ME FOR IT. BUT I ALSO KNEW THAT SUCH A CALLING NOT ONLY INVITED ME INTO RADICAL DEPENDENCE UPON HIM, BUT ALSO INTO A RADICAL DEPENDENCE UPON OTHERS IN THE BODY OF CHRIST.

A kind of two-way radical dependence was necessary: vertical dependence upon God and horizontal dependence upon God's people. In this chapter, we'll start by examining the critical nature of vertical dependence.

RADICAL VERTICAL DEPENDENCE

Over the years that I've been in ministry, I have often had people remark to me, "I know I need to get right with God." Generally, what they mean when they say this is that they need to get their act together behaviorally. Stop doing bad or destructive things. Become more religiously committed. Quit a bad habit. Be more self-controlled. Be less angry. But this deep longing to "get right" or "be better" will never come from these self-dependent measures. In this life, in these

---

bodies, with hearts and minds marred by sin, we will never be able to get it right on our own. We will always fall short (Romans 3:23). As stated in chapter 1, the true transformation our hearts long for is only found in radical dependence upon the Lord. We need God to do what only he can do to *make* and *keep* us right. This transformation can only happen through Jesus' righteousness being imputed to us. A deep dependence upon Christ, to be for us everything we're not, is what the Bible calls faith, or trust. And that trust—that faith—is expressed through what I'm calling a radical, "vertical" dependence upon him.

The Scriptures show us time and time again that God is the only one who deserves our complete trust and our exclusive worship. In Old Testament times, God's people would remind each other of this in the songs or psalms they would sing to "preach" the truth to themselves. One group of these psalms—what we know as Psalms 120 through 134—were songs that God's people would sing as they made their pilgrimages to Jerusalem for annual festivals. From various places throughout Israel, God's people would make their way to the temple, high on Mount Zion in the Holy City. These psalms are known as the "Songs of Ascent" because they would sing these songs as they ascended to the temple. As God's people sang them, the words would remind them of who God is, who they were, and why he alone deserved their worship and their trust.

Here is one of those songs:

I lift up my eyes to the hills.
  From where does my help come?
My help comes from the LORD,
  who made heaven and earth.
He will not let your foot be moved;
  he who keeps you will not slumber.
Behold, he who keeps Israel
  will neither slumber nor sleep.
The LORD *is your keeper;*
  the LORD *is your shade on your right hand.*
The sun shall not strike you by day,
  nor the moon by night.

The LORD will keep you from all evil;
  he will keep your life.
The LORD will keep
  your going out and your coming in
  from this time forth and forevermore.
(Psalm 121)

The journey toward Jerusalem was not an easy one. Threats and challenges could confront the traveler at any turn. The terrain could be treacherous. Sudden storms might come. On lonely stretches, robbers might lay in wait. This was especially true of the road between Jericho and Jerusalem. Often called the "Way of Blood," this road was nestled in the deep valleys of the Judean desert and served as the main thoroughfare between the two ancient cities. Travelers would journey in fear knowing that around the next corner, or in the rock clefts above, there could be robbers ready to pounce. Any Jew traveling westward from Jericho to Jerusalem on this road was sure to pass by altars with idols of false gods tucked into the steep hillsides. These idols were created and placed there by neighboring nations to serve as protection and a source of solace for anxious travelers. Although God's people ascending to Jerusalem knew that these idols had no real power, you can imagine how enticing their presence—in countless caves, crevices, and folds along the way—would have been to them as they journeyed on.

Think about it … these false gods of the hills promised all manner of safety, protection, and provision that felt close and within reach. I'm sure more than a few of God's people bought into their lies (or at least stopped to pay their respects to these false gods "just in case"), but Psalm 121 was meant to remind them that their help came not from the man-made idols tucked into the hills, but from the Maker of the hills himself!

On the steep, rocky roads to Jerusalem, the song declares that the God of Israel will not allow your feet to slip or to stumble. No need to sacrifice to the idols of sure-footedness or safety. The God of Israel keeps his people upright. And Israel's God never sleeps, so his children can rest in confidence. No need to worship the gods of the sun or the moon—the God of Israel created and commands them both. He will protect his own in the harsh light of day and in the deepest dark of night. He will keep you and preserve you, this traveling psalm says—not just today, on this road, but "from this time forth, and forevermore."

In other words, you can depend upon him always, for everything.

It's critically important that we see and believe this. The struggle God's people had in that day with the idols of the hills mirrors our own struggle with contemporary idols of the heart!

We are tempted by nearby idols too. The temptation to turn to the false gods of wealth, success, and reputation can feel overwhelming. In a world that feels so chaotic and unsure, we can easily turn to the idols of power and control. And when the pain, monotony, and fear of life sets in, is there anything we have come to desire more than the mindless escape our phones and tablets perpetually offer? We imagine these things will help us and ultimately satisfy us, but the more we give ourselves to them, the more they leave us wanting more. The idols of the hills for the Israelites were tempting because they seemed so tangible. So visible. So near. They must have felt more accessible to them than God did. In the moment, they seemed to promise so much more than the perceptibly distant God of their fathers.

Like those long-ago Jews traveling to Jerusalem, we are people on the way too. We may not be traveling a daunting ancient road called the "Way of Blood," but we're traveling the tumultuous and rocky roads of life, which are littered with idols that beckon our hearts. Just like those ancient idols, they promise the safety we long for and the surety we crave. They seduce with promises of pleasure and fulfillment. But just like chocolate covered dog food, they aren't what they seem. They won't sustain us. They will not keep us.

Six times in Psalm 121 the psalmist said that God is our keeper. You and I know today what those ancient travelers did not: that the way God keeps us is through his Son, Jesus. In him all the plans of God unfold. He is the One who fulfills every promise of God to his people, Jew and Gentile alike.

The gospel of John tells us that Jesus is the Good Shepherd who will not let his sheep fall away:

*"I am the good shepherd. I know my own and my own know me, just as the Father knows me and I know the Father; and I lay down my life for the sheep ... My sheep hear my voice, and I know them, and they follow me. I give them eternal life, and they will never perish, and **no one will snatch them out of my hand.** My Father, who has given them to me, is greater than all, and **no one is able to snatch them out of the Father's hand."***
(John 10:14–15, 27–29, emphasis added)

If you are a follower of Christ, there is no better place for you to be than in the hands of Jesus, our Shepherd, our Keeper. As our Keeper, Jesus reassures us that his followers are not only kept secure in his hands, but also in the hands of the Father. Just a few chapters later in John 16, he offers us even more security as our Keeper by promising that he will send us a Helper—the Holy Spirit of God. It is the Holy Spirit who empowers us, fills us, and seals us for the day of redemption, guaranteeing our inheritance (Ephesians 1:13–14). In every way, we are kept. We are held steadfastly in the secure hands and help of our Triune God.

The people of Israel could only look past the hills to see their God. But we can look inside. The Spirit dwells within us, helping us to see and recognize the nearness of the Father and the Son. We may be tempted to run to the hills in search of idols, thinking that they will keep us. But the help we need is closer, indeed it dwells within us.

I'll give you an example of an alluring "nearby idol" that is front and center in our home right now, especially with our teenagers. I mentioned it earlier. It's commonly called "screen time." That ever-present screen—as near as our fingertips—is constantly pinging and beckoning with texts, IMs, DMs, and videos from an ever-changing array of apps like Instagram, TikTok, and Snapchat. (I'm sure that by the time you read this those apps will be obsolete, and some new ones will have taken the digital world by storm!)

Although we fight to manage their devices closely, our kids want to run to those "digital hills" all the time. And before you think I'm only going to throw this on my kids, Rachel and I are guilty as well. As adults we are certainly not immune! (Our digital hill idols are probably more in the line of Facebook and Twitter!) The screen-time idol screams to us that our worth is tied to the number of likes, comments, retweets, and reposts we get—that the responses and approval of others somehow prove our worth. We race to find our identity and worth in fickle and false "likes" when the faithful and true love of God is knocking at the door. There are many things that are waging war for the affections of our hearts; but parents, don't be lured into the temptation of believing that your child's screen time is a benign time-saver or babysitter. Fight to do the hard work of engaging with your child face-to-face and heart-to-heart. Considering all that can be brought into the life and mind of a child through a screen, there may be no more important idol for parents to ferociously fight.

If we're not radically dependent upon God, we will quickly run to an idol, and not to the Keeper of our hearts. We will depend on "followers" instead of following the Good Shepherd. We will look to the screen for direction and worth, instead of looking to Christ and listening for the Holy Spirit as he speaks to us a better word. That's how idolatry works.

Idolatry is as old as time. It's the central player in the human heart that is naturally at war with God. This is why the first two commandments that God gave Moses on Mount Sinai dealt with this very issue. Let's consider now the "path" that idolatry often takes as it robs our hearts of radical dependence upon the Lord.

QUESTIONS FOR REFLECTION

1. Can you articulate in your own words what it means to have "radical vertical dependence"?

2. Looking back at Psalm 121, what modern-day idols tempt you along your journey? How do the words of the psalmist guide your heart back on course?

3. When you consider the false gods of wealth, success, and reputation, does one of these idols resonate with your heart? Is there something not listed that you often run to for comfort or security?

4. As we reflect on John 10, how does the reality that Jesus is your Good Shepherd bring you strength and confidence for the journey ahead?

5. "If we're not radically dependent upon God, we will quickly run to an idol, and not to the Keeper of our hearts." Are there idols you are currently running to instead of to Jesus, the Keeper of your heart? Is there a specific instance, habit, or life pattern you need to confess to God right now?

CHAPTER 3

THE PATH OF IDOLATRY

NO MATTER THE IDOL—WHETHER IT'S WEALTH, SEX, STATUS, COMFORT, REPUTATION, PERFORMANCE, POSSESSIONS, OR SOMETHING ELSE—IDOLATRY ALWAYS FOLLOWS A PATTERN. WHEN WE RECOGNIZE THE PATTERN, WE CAN CHANGE DIRECTION AND, WITH THE HOLY SPIRIT'S POWER, AVOID THE DESTRUCTIVE END OF IDOLATRY.

> ## THE PATH OF IDOLATRY:
>
> Distraction
> Dreaming
> Desperation
> Dependence
> **Disillusionment**
> **Destruction**

Idolatry typically begins with **distraction**. We are by nature a distracted people, perpetually looking around, searching for the things we most long for and finding ourselves distracted by their "just out of reach" allure. Then our distraction turns to **dreaming** as we imagine the pleasure or comfort or security of those longed-for things. In time, our dreaming becomes **desperation**. We convince ourselves that we *must* have that thing we long for. In time, our desperation results in actual possession of the desired thing or status. Naturally, once possessed, we experience increasing **dependence** upon that desired thing to give us satisfaction and meet our felt needs. But whatever the idol might be, it doesn't ultimately provide what we thought it would—and so we become **disillusioned**. As disillusionment takes further root, the natural end of the path of idolatry is **destruction**.

You might read that word *destruction* and think that it's a bit extreme. It's not. I use that word purposefully, because that's exactly what idols do to us over time. Our chronic dependence upon something to give us what only God can give will end in spiritual and sometimes physical and emotional destruction, depending on the nature of the idol being clung to.

On this idolatrous path, hope is destroyed. Health and homes and relationships may be destroyed. But it doesn't have to be that way. Because there's an exit on the path of idolatry that leads to the way of radical dependence, not upon an idol, but upon God. Not only are we a naturally distracted people, we are also a naturally dependent people. We will depend on something or someone no matter what. The question isn't, "*Will* we be dependent?" The question is "What or whom will we be dependent upon?"

When our distraction and dreaming sends us searching for the object of our longing; when our desperation says we *must* have it, we can shift our focus from our idols of choice to God. We can look for his intervening grace in our lives, depending not on those things in the hills of our hearts, but on him. As we begin to do that (not perfectly, but slowly and surely) we find ourselves trusting him more, even radically depending upon him. We may still look to other things, but we will more readily see how those things lead to disappointment and destruction when depended on in the place of God.

Allowing him to lead us back like the Good Shepherd he is, we confess to him that although we've strayed, we want to depend on him and him alone. We don't want to trust the idols of the hills. We want to look past them to the God who *made* the hills. By taking this exit, we avoid the disillusionment and destruction of the path of idolatry. By his grace, we begin to **dispossess** our idols and increasingly **delight** in him! We come to understand that the path of radical dependence on God is the better way: it's the path of life!

We begin to experience the fullness of who Jesus is: "*I am the way, and the truth, and the life. No one comes to the Father except through me*" (John 14:6). On this path of ever-growing delight, we find joy in his presence and discover that at his right hand are pleasures forevermore (Psalm 16:11).

Which will it be? The way of destruction in the hands of unfaithful idols? Or the way of delight in the hands of a faithful God?

We sing the doxology at the end of every worship service at Perimeter Church. It begins with the words "Praise God from whom all blessings flow." It's a kind of anti-idolatry statement that's meant to press us into dependence upon the God who keeps us. John Witvliet says, "Every time we sing praise to the triune God, we are asserting our opposition to anything that would attempt to stand in God's place."[1] Self-made gods won't do. Worldly idols won't cut it. We are waging war against those. "When we sing 'Praise God from whom all blessings flow,' we are also saying 'Down with the gods from whom *no* blessings flow.'"[2]

QUESTIONS FOR REFLECTION

1. When you consider the "Path of Idolatry," do you agree with this progression? How have you seen it played out in areas of your own life?

2. What distractions in your life must you keep in check in order for you to not slip down this idolatry path?

3. "Our chronic dependence upon something to give us what only God can give will end in spiritual and sometimes physical and emotional destruction, depending on the nature of the idol being clung to." Do you believe this is true? Why or why not?

4. What pivotal actions must you take to change your path to a path of dependence, resulting in delight in Jesus? What might this look like in your life?

5. As you consider the words of the Doxology, how is the singing of these words waging war against the idols of this world?

CHAPTER 4

ROOTED IN RADICAL HORIZONTAL DEPENDENCE

RADICAL VERTICAL DEPENDENCE IS ESSENTIAL TO OUR WELL-BEING AS INDIVIDUALS AND AS A CHURCH. BUT WE NEED RADICAL HORIZONTAL DEPENDENCE, TOO. WE NEED EACH OTHER.

In the first twelve verses of Mark chapter 2, a profound story is recorded for us. It was early in Jesus' ministry, and he had already reached a sort of rock star status, if you will. Huge crowds were following him everywhere he went as he performed miracle after miracle while proclaiming that the kingdom of God was at hand. The news had spread that Jesus was preaching and teaching in a home in the small fishing village of Capernaum. So many had come to hear him that it was standing room only in and around the house! Not one more person could get in the door, but four men had a friend who desperately needed Jesus. This friend was paralyzed, and there was only One who could heal him. So, they did what you would logically expect them to do ... they dug through the roof of the home and lowered him in. They didn't just drop a note or whistle to get everyone's attention. No, they dug a man-sized hole through a mud and thatch roof. Picture this: They were disassembling the roof of this home *while Jesus was teaching*. Pieces of the roof were falling in, and he didn't stop them. They placed their friend who was completely dependent and could not move at the feet of Jesus, and then they depended upon Jesus to do the rest.

When Jesus saw their act of mercy and faith he said to the man, "Son, your sins are forgiven." Needless to say, this caused quite a stir among the onlooking religious elite. No one can forgive sins but God alone! The crowd marveled at this man who was claiming to be God in their midst. It's at this point that I imagine that the paralytic might have said, "Thanks, but I'm still paralyzed!" What Jesus did next astonished the crowd even more. In order to prove that he had the authority to forgive sins, he healed the paralytic. Before they knew it, the paralytic was picking up his own mat and walking with his friends out of the home. A tremendous account that carries with it significant implications regarding the divinity and mission of Christ. But for the sake of the focus of this chapter, I want to zoom in on the faith and the love of the paralytic's friends.

What the people witnessed that day was radical horizontal dependence within the body of Christ. They saw a tangible expression of loving care that refused to let a member of their community remain in distress but ushered him into the presence of Christ. This man's friends took drastic measures to carry a sick brother to the feet of Jesus.

Maybe you've been on the receiving end of that kind of horizontal dependence. I know for a fact I have. I often tell people that Hattiesburg, Mississippi, was the place God took me to humble me.

In 2002, Rachel and I moved to Hattiesburg on our first assignment with Cru (Campus Crusade for Christ). I was a twenty-two-year-old, newly married, overconfident man when we arrived there. We were sent to reignite a fledgling campus ministry at the University of Southern Mississippi. I was giving it everything I had, but the ministry and life I had envisioned in Hattiesburg wasn't coming together. Part of it was that I had set unrealistic expectations that were centered more on selfish ambition than on healthy growth. We also struggled finding community and felt isolated in a city that was very culturally different from what we were used to. I soon found myself deep in the throes of anxiety and depression. And when I say deep, I mean *deep*.

I could barely make it from the bedroom to the couch each morning, and some days I couldn't even manage to get out of bed. If I had known how to pull myself out of that abyss—and I didn't—I wouldn't have had the emotional, physical, or spiritual strength to try. But I had a loving wife and community around me who carried me to the feet of Jesus. They wouldn't let me stay where I was. Through their prayers, encouragement, and even through medical intervention and education, they brought me to Jesus not unlike the friends of the paralytic—and slowly but surely, he did his healing work in me.

We live in a highly consumeristic and individualistic church culture in America. Today's church climate scarcely encourages dependence of any kind. Comfort, convenience, and independence are championed. The "don't let them see you cry" false bravado of yesteryear has too often defined masculinity in the church. Admission of weakness and frailty can carry with it an unshakable stigma. But who is the church for if not the weak? And who are the weak if not all of us?

Much has been written about the church's unbiblical disposition to present herself as a place where one must be "put together" to participate, so I won't belabor that point. I'll simply say that the world needs the church. The world needs a church full of people who mimic the friends of the paralytic. A people unwavering in their love for one another. A people committed to helping one another in our weaknesses to find the encouragement, power, solace, and rest that is only found in Jesus.

God created us to experience him in the context of community and the local church is *his* community. We must fight hard against the cultural current and become rooted in radical horizontal dependence. Together we are to take each other to Jesus in prayer, in encouragement, in service to one another, and ultimately in loving one another. This gospel-rich love displayed in and through the church is a love that persists regardless of socioeconomic status, ethnicity, or political affiliation. We need Jesus, yes. But we also need each other!

I alluded to this in the forward of this book, but it seems to me that after a year like 2020 there's no better time for the church to be the church. In a year that brought us a pandemic, death of friends and family, economic crisis, social and political unrest, and a divisiveness that won't soon be remedied, people are deeply feeling the brokenness and cruelty of this world perhaps like never before in our lifetimes. Isolation and chaos, although undesired, now serve as a foundation for many to find hope in the arms of Jesus, through his body—the church.

And so, we need to be rooted. Rooted to flourish in a time such as this.

By developing our roots in prayer, repentance, self-denial and sacrifice, obedience, discipleship, forgiveness and generosity, and thanksgiving, we can become a radically dependent people ... a radically dependent church.

QUESTIONS FOR REFLECTION

1. Is the idea of "Radical Horizontal Dependence" new to you? As you consider your background and upbringing, were you raised to see horizontal dependence as acceptable or as a sign of weakness? If you were raised in the church, was horizontal dependence taught as being just as important for our spiritual lives as vertical dependence?

2. As you consider the story of the paralytic, is there a time in your life in which you could relate to this type of spiritual paralysis? Have you ever been paralyzed by anxiety, an addiction, or maybe even the approval of others?

3. Are there friends in your life you would feel comfortable reaching out to in a season of spiritual paralysis? Can you remember a scenario in which you were that type of friend?

4. "God created us to experience him in the context of community, and the local church is his community." Are you part of a local church? Has your experience been like the community described above? If so , are there changes you need to make to the type of church you are part of or possibly to your commitment level to your present church? How might you be part of the change you long to see in your church?

5. How might a radically dependent church give the utmost glory to God by showing his character and power to a watching world?

CHAPTER 5

ROOTED IN PRAYER

FOR THIS REASON I BOW MY KNEES BEFORE THE
FATHER, FROM WHOM EVERY FAMILY IN HEAVEN
AND ON EARTH IS NAMED, THAT ACCORDING
TO THE RICHES OF HIS GLORY, HE MAY GRANT
YOU TO BE STRENGTHENED WITH POWER
THROUGH HIS SPIRIT IN YOUR INNER BEING,
SO THAT CHRIST MAY DWELL IN YOUR HEARTS
THROUGH FAITH—THAT YOU, BEING ROOTED
AND GROUNDED IN LOVE, MAY HAVE STRENGTH
TO COMPREHEND WITH ALL THE SAINTS WHAT
IS THE BREADTH AND LENGTH AND HEIGHT AND
DEPTH, AND TO KNOW THE LOVE OF CHRIST
THAT SURPASSES KNOWLEDGE, THAT YOU MAY
BE FILLED WITH ALL THE FULLNESS OF GOD.

(EPHESIANS 3:14-19)

I don't know all that God has planned for Perimeter Church, but I do know this: we will remain a church centered on the Word of God, and we will always be a church that prays. I'm convinced that a lifestyle of radical dependence upon the Lord is first and foremost a lifestyle rooted in prayer, because prayer is the tangible expression of a dependent heart. If you asked me to describe our church twenty, thirty, or forty years from now, I would say with great expectation that we will be a people of God, radically dependent upon him to do what only he can do in and through us for his glory. As radically dependent people, we will be a people of prayer.

Here's a corollary to that: pastors are radically dependent people too. Therefore pastors must pray! Biblically speaking, my role as a pastor here is primarily threefold: teach the Word of God, shepherd

---

God's flock, and pray. The first two responsibilities come more naturally to me as an extrovert who is energized by people and who loves to shepherd others toward Jesus. The third critical responsibility does not come as naturally to me. Prayer can feel far more challenging than preaching. Prayer is hard work. Prayer sometimes seems less practical than other things on our "must-do" lists, but in truth, prayer is the most critically important work we can do.

Why do I say this? Because of the powerful example of the first century Church recorded in the book of Acts and the letters of Paul; because of the historic examples of the great revival movements of the Church; and because of the personal, passionate example of the Lord Jesus Christ himself.

THE EARLY CHURCH PRAYED

The book of Acts—short for Acts of the Apostles—records the earliest history of the Church. Acts begins where the Gospels end: Jesus was crucified and rose from the dead. He appeared in the region of Galilee for forty days and more than five hundred people witnessed his post-resurrection presence. He gave final instructions to his followers (Matthew 28:19–20) and ascended into heaven, telling his disciples to wait in Jerusalem for *"the gift my Father promised, which you have heard me speak about"* (Acts 1:4 NIV).

While they were waiting for that gift, the promised Holy Spirit, *"they all joined together constantly in prayer"* (Acts 1:14 NIV). The disciples prayed. The women who had followed Jesus to the cross prayed. His mother Mary and his brothers prayed. They prayed for the coming Holy Spirit. They prayed for guidance from God to add a disciple to replace Judas and they selected Matthias. Then, on the day of Pentecost as they were gathered to pray, *"a sound like the blowing of a violent wind came from heaven and filled the whole house where they were sitting"* (Acts 2:2 NIV). All who were there were filled with the Holy Spirit, just as the Lord had promised.

Other Jews gathering in Jerusalem at the same time for the feast of Pentecost witnessed this miracle, and Peter preached to them about Jesus. Thousands believed in him, repented, and were baptized.

They received the Holy Spirit too. Then the writer of Acts said that all of these new believers in Jesus *"devoted themselves to the apostles' teaching and to fellowship, to the breaking of bread and to prayer"* (Acts 2:42 NIV).

Not long after this, Peter and John—going up to the temple at the time of prayer—healed a man waiting at the temple gate. The healing drew a crowd, and Peter began to preach. More people were saved, and the chief priests and elders summoned Peter and John and commanded them to stop talking about Jesus. They refused. "Sorry. No can do, guys." They were threatened and released and returned to their friends to report what had happened. Then, as you might expect, they all prayed.

The task before them to "go and make disciples" was great. The resistance was, too. They weren't skilled speakers or teachers. They were ordinary men, dependent on God to fill and equip them. So they prayed and kept on praying.

They prayed as they appointed deacons (Acts 6:1–7). They prayed as they sent out missionaries (Acts 13:1–3; 15:40). They prayed and fasted as they appointed elders during their missionary journeys (Acts 14:21–23). As they prayed in jail cells, doors sprung open and their jailers became followers of Christ (Acts 16:22–34). They prayed, and the church grew (Acts 2:42–47; 4:31–35; 5:12–14; 5:42; 6:7; 8:14–17; 9:31). Leaders prayed and exhorted others to pray (Acts 4:31; 6:4; 2 Timothy 1:3).

The Apostle Paul encouraged his Christian brothers in Rome to be *"fervent in spirit ... rejoice in hope, be patient in tribulation, be constant in prayer"* (Romans 12:11–12).

To the Ephesian Christians he wrote, *"[pray] at all times in the Spirit, with all prayer and supplication. To that end, keep alert with all perseverance, making supplication for all the saints, and also for me, that words may be given to me in opening my mouth boldly to proclaim the mystery of the gospel"* (Ephesians 6:18–19).

He advised the Philippian church to *"not be anxious about anything, but in everything by prayer and supplication with thanksgiving let your requests be made known to God. And the peace of God, which surpasses all understanding, will guard your hearts and your minds in Christ Jesus"* (Philippians 4:6–7).

And to the Thessalonians Paul wrote, *"Rejoice always, pray without ceasing, give thanks in all circumstances; for this is the will of God in Christ Jesus for you"* (1 Thessalonians 5:16–18). The Scriptures make it clear: The earliest Church was a praying church from the beginning.

THE CHURCH THROUGH HISTORY HAS PRAYED

From its earliest days and throughout the history of the Church, God has birthed renewal and awakening in her over and over again from the trenches of prayer. Here are a few quick highlights:

In Europe, the First Great Awakening began in 1727 in now modern-day Germany among a praying Moravian community called Herrnhut. These believers gathered and prayed around the clock for one hundred years—yes, you read that correctly—for the reviving and spread of God's church throughout Europe.

In America, the First Great Awakening of the 1730s and 1740s in New England was birthed out of Jonathan Edwards's call to "concerts of prayer" similar to the prayer outpourings begun in Scotland and Great Britain a few years before.

The Second Great Awakening in the early 1800s came out of another movement of prayer and lasted for the first several decades of the nineteenth century.

The Modern Missionary Movement of the nineteenth century began with five college students who gathered to pray under a haystack during a thunderstorm in 1806.

The Scottish Hebrides Revival, which swept through the islands of Scotland's west coast from 1949 to 1952, sprang from the prayers of two elderly women and seven men who committed to pray twice a week in a local barn.

The Businessman's Revival—the last great nationwide revival movement in U.S. history—began with a six-man prayer meeting in lower Manhattan in September of 1857. A month later, the Panic of 1857 struck financial markets, putting thousands out of work. The six-man meeting multiplied to ten thousand men in a matter of months and soon spread to other cities, filling churches across the country up to three times a day ... *for prayer.*

Prayer has played a crucial role in the life of Perimeter Church, too, beginning long before I arrived on the scene. Perimeter's founding pastor, Randy Pope, tells how, in the early 1990s, the church was seeking to secure a place for a permanent home in the north Atlanta area. "We knew the amount of acreage we needed," he says, "and we had two commercial Realtors in our church who researched available properties for us. Only one piece of property met our stated criteria, and it happened to be the number one piece of land in the area. We were told it was already under contract—a good contract—and for three times more than we were willing to pay."

Randy asked the church to pray, and then asked the Realtors representing Perimeter to go back to the property owner and present our best offer. They did and were essentially escorted out the door and told we weren't even in the ballpark with our number. But the church and its leaders continued to pray for several more weeks. Then Randy asked our agents to go back to the seller (whose prior deal had not closed) and present our offer again.

This time, they were met with a stunning reception. "Do you still want our property?" they were asked. They confirmed that Perimeter did, in fact, still want the land, but at the same offered price. "If you can arrange your financing by this date," they were told, "we will accept your offer." And with that the deal was done.

Later Randy learned that one of the most powerful women in that community—the leader of a consortium of nearly forty nearby homeowners' associations—had walked the property for a number of years, praying that God would not let it be sold to anyone except a buyer who would use it for God's glory. She was fifty-eight years old and had come to Christ ten years before. She knew Perimeter's reputation and advocated with surrounding homeowners for us, saying we were the ones who should develop it.

Our congregation's prayers, and even the prayers of a stranger, brought us to the home Perimeter Church occupies today, and those prayers have enabled us to share the gospel and love our city in Jesus' name for twenty-five years now.

These examples convince me that you would be hard pressed to find a revival movement of God anywhere, at any time, in the Church's history that wasn't begun by people who prayed desperately for God to show up and do what only he can do in the hearts of his people.

In each of these examples, ordinary people depended upon God, called upon his name, and cried out to him in prayer. They declared their reliance upon him and asked him, by his power and for his glory, to move in the hearts of men and women. And he did.

JESUS PRAYED ... AND IS PRAYING

These examples are powerful, but there's one truth about prayer that convicts me like no other: *even the Lord Jesus himself prayed!* Throughout the Gospels we see example after example of Christ praying. Have you ever wondered about this? Why would Jesus pray? He's God in the flesh, the beloved Son of the Father. As a man, he walked in sinless perfection, utterly in tune with God's will. So why would he or should he pray? John chapter 5 gives us the answer. After he was challenged by the religious elite of the day for healing on the Sabbath (the Jews had specific laws against "working" on this day), Jesus responded to their protests by saying, *"My Father is working until now, and I am working"* (John 5:17). In other words, "I'm doing what I see my Father is doing, and what he tells me to do."

Jesus didn't come to earth to fulfill his own agenda. He came to advance his Father's plan. *"Truly, truly, I say to you,"* Jesus told them, *"the Son can do nothing of his own accord, but only what he sees the Father doing. For whatever the Father does, that the Son does likewise. For the Father loves the Son and shows him all that he himself is doing. And greater works than these will he show him, so that you may marvel"* (John 5:19–20).

Jesus, who walked in close intimacy with the Father, looked constantly to him for guidance and was committed to doing only what the Father willed—nothing more, nothing less. Though sinless, he "learned obedience" as he constantly sought to do the Father's will (Hebrews 5:7–10, esp. v.8, John 4:34). Indeed, Jesus repeatedly declared, that he could do nothing on his own authority and sought not his own will but the will of God (John 5:30; 6:38; 8:28–29, 42). Jesus lived to reveal the Father (as should we all) as if he were putting the Father on constant display (John 12:45; 14:8–9), saying only what he heard the

Father saying and doing only what he saw the Father doing (John 8:26; 10:17–18, 37–38; 12:49–50).

In the garden of Gethsemane Jesus wrestled in prayer before the Father, going against his very human desire as the cross came into view. Jesus struggled with what was before him. Falling on his knees in agony he prayed, *"Father, if you are willing, remove this cup from me. Nevertheless, not my will, but yours, be done"* (Luke 22:42). In his most dire moment, we see the Son submitting to and depending on the Father. Here is Jesus—the God-man—exercising full dependence upon the Father. Jesus, the perfect image of God, who came to rescue marred image bearers, modeled for us how redeemed image bearers are to pray.

If Jesus prayed to follow the will of the Father, how much more should I? If Jesus refused to move without being certain of the Father's intention, what makes me think I can manage without that assurance? 1 Thessalonians 5:17–18 says to *"pray without ceasing, give thanks in all circumstances; for this is the will of God in Christ Jesus for you."* God wants me to be a person of never-ceasing prayer, giving thanks to him in all circumstances. Sometimes we wrestle over God's will for our lives as we seek to understand where he is leading. But sometimes, God plainly lays out for us what his will is for how we are to live. Whatever else God's will for us may hold, it begins here: to pray without ceasing and to give thanks in all circumstances.

And what does it mean to pray without ceasing? Does it mean we are consciously praying every moment of every day? Well, no. That would be impossible. But it does mean that the posture of our hearts is one of continual communion with and dependence upon God. As we go through our days doing what God has called us to do, we are to be in an attitude of dependence, flowing from a heart turned toward God, expressing itself through frequent prayer.

Jesus prayed this way and is praying still. One of the beautiful realities of the gospel is not just that Jesus died for our sins and rose from the dead. He did these things, yes! But he also ascended into heaven where he sits at the right hand of God the Father and—get this—continues to pray for you and me! Jesus prayed constantly during his time on earth, and Hebrews 7 tells us that as our High

Priest, he is still interceding today (Hebrews 2:14–18; 4:14–16; 7:25; Romans 8:26–28, 34). I get chills when I think of this. **Jesus is praying for me.** The resurrected Son of God is bringing my name before the throne of the Father.

If you're a follower of Jesus he is praying for you, too. Don't you want to get in on that? I wonder about what he is saying over me, what he has planned for me. I don't want to miss it. Whatever prayer Jesus, in the fullness of the Spirit, is praying on my behalf, I want to echo it. Prayer is fundamentally about God aligning my heart to his, not his heart to mine. I want to be able to pray with Jesus, "Not my will, but yours, be done." I want to want what he wants for me!

We are to be a people who pray to know and follow the Father's will, just as Jesus did.

PRAYER IS PRACTICAL

I've had so many conversations with folks about prayer. One of the things I often hear is that prayer can be difficult—and I agree. I struggle with it, too. The other thing I hear is that prayer just doesn't seem practical, compared with other things we might do. Here, I have to disagree.

I've come to believe that prayer is one of the most practical things I can do. With what can feel like a million things on my plate any given day, the temptation is constant to busy myself with endless work. After all, it's kingdom work, right? But as Oswald Chambers once famously wrote, "Prayer does not fit us for the greater work, prayer is the greater work."[3] Puritan pastor John Owen takes the stakes up a notch. Owen said, "A minister may fill his pews, his communion roll, the mouths of the public, but what that minister is **on his knees in secret before God Almighty**, that he is and no more."[4] Prayer is a high calling, and one I want to do my best to lead others in.

I'm fully aware that where prayer is concerned, I will be leading not only from my strengths but also from my weaknesses. You and I will be in this thing together, rooting ourselves in prayer—whether we feel adequate for the task or not. It doesn't matter if you feel like you're "good" at prayer. It doesn't matter if you're a beginner or if you come to prayer with a lifetime of faithful practice. Wherever you are in your spiritual journey, I'm urging you to become a person who radically depends upon the Lord in prayer.

The First Century Church prayed. The global Church has continued to pray. Jesus never ceased praying and prays today. And prayer is practical. Why do I say practical? Because prayer does these three very practical things:

1. Prayer helps us to see God rightly.

2. Prayer helps us to see ourselves rightly.

3. Prayer helps us see others and our circumstances rightly.

The more we pray, the more we see God as he really is. When we pray, Tim Keller says, we encounter God. We know "the awe of praising his glory, the intimacy of finding his grace, and the struggle of asking his help, all of which can lead us to know the spiritual reality of his presence."[5] The more we pray, the more we encounter God, learn his character, and experience his presence.

Also, the more we pray, the more we see ourselves rightly. The intimacy of prayer opens the deep vault of our hearts, helping us to both see and acknowledge our sins, and receive God's grace and forgiveness. (Two more "roots" of dependence we'll explore in the next chapters.) The Christian who consistently prays is unlikely to think of himself or herself too highly or to become stuck in a cycle of shame or self-condemnation. In prayer, we commune with a forgiving, gracious, compassionate, loving, merciful, and good God, and we receive from him forgiveness, grace, compassion, love, and mercy. His love both exposes us and changes us.

Finally, the more we pray, the more God begins to give us the eyes of Jesus to see others and our circumstances as they really are. We gain "the mind of Christ" as we spend time in God's presence. His priorities become our priorities. We come to love what he loves, and to reject what he rejects. Over time, we may even find ourselves naturally responding to difficult people and circumstances as he would, not as we might be prone to do in our own flesh.

I know the rhythms and demands of twenty-first century life are not exactly conducive to prayer. We are a busy and distracted people in a culture that glorifies busyness. Even the Church is not exempt; missionally engaging in the world around us often means our busy schedules get even busier! But we can't wait for a "better time" to pray. The world around us is always going to be busy, and busyness will always be a challenge to prayer. But the choice to pray isn't dictated by the world around us, it's made in our hearts. Prayer is hard. We are busy. We must choose to pray anyway.

Embracing a lifestyle of radically dependent prayer can feel like we're sacrificing a lot, and in some ways, we are. But any sacrifice you and I make to spend time in prayer pales in comparison to the good we gain by doing so. In his book, *A Praying Life*, Paul Miller writes, "What do I lose when I have a praying life? Control. Independence. What do I gain? Friendship with God. A quiet heart. The living work of God in the hearts of those I love. The ability to roll back the tide of evil. Essentially, I lose my kingdom and get his. I move from being an independent player to a dependent lover. I move from being an orphan to a child of God."[6]

May you and I be people who gladly make this trade! May we, with the help of God, exchange our desire for control and independence for a lifestyle of radical dependence, rooted deeply in prayer. May we be absolutely convinced that there is *nothing* we can do apart from God (John 15:5). And may we be amazed and enthralled with the reality that we are invited into communion with the God of the universe, who longs to do in us *"immeasurably more than all we ask or imagine"* (Ephesians 3:20 NIV).

QUESTIONS FOR REFLECTION

1. What adjectives would you use to describe your experience with prayer? Taking an honest inventory of this aspect of your spiritual life, what are your greatest joys and frustrations with prayer?

2. "Prayer is the most critically important work we can do."
Do you believe this statement to be true? If so, in what ways does your prayer life support this belief or discredit it?

3. In what ways do we see the early church completely reliant on prayer? Can you recount a moment in your own life that God answered your prayers in an extraordinary way?

4. When you consider the present reality that Jesus is interceding on your behalf each moment, what assurance does this give your heart? How does this assurance affect your own prayer life?

5. As we consider that Paul asked God to do "immeasurably more than all we ask or imagine," what needs in your own life or the lives of others should you take to God, believing his grace and power to be sufficient for every need?

CHAPTER 6

ROOTED IN REPENTANCE

HAVE MERCY ON ME, O GOD, ACCORDING TO YOUR STEADFAST LOVE; ACCORDING TO YOUR ABUNDANT MERCY BLOT OUT MY TRANSGRESSIONS. WASH ME THOROUGHLY FROM MY INIQUITY, AND CLEANSE ME FROM MY SIN! FOR I KNOW MY TRANSGRESSIONS, AND MY SIN IS EVER BEFORE ME. AGAINST YOU, YOU ONLY, HAVE I SINNED AND DONE WHAT IS EVIL IN YOUR SIGHT.

(PSALM 51:1-4)

Have you ever done something blatantly wrong and then denied it? I mean willfully and with full knowledge sinned, and then—probably because you were caught red-handed—insisted that you were not guilty?

Anyone?

If you can't identify, either your memory is fading, or you're flat out lying!

The sin-and-denial cycle is a part of the human experience. Young or old, we're naturals at it. We sin, and then say we didn't or insist that it was someone else's fault. We go to great lengths to defend ourselves, and only when we're trapped beyond any hope of escape do we relent. Even those of us who are Christians bear an age-old residue of self-protection and pride that causes us to deny our wrongdoing. Thanks to our ancestors, Adam and Eve, we're crafty deniers, constantly battling with our old nature and defaulting into disobedience.

We're a people who struggle deeply with seeing our sin, calling it sin, confessing it, and turning from it—a process the Bible calls *repentance*.

Repentance is another key "root" in our lifestyle of radical dependence. By God's grace he calls us to look honestly at the fault lines in our own hearts, surrendering our pride for humility and our denial for sincere confession and renewal.

THE ANATOMY OF REPENTANCE

There's a structure to repentance that helps us know whether it is true or false, counterfeit or genuine. This "anatomy of repentance" involves three things: an admission of wrong, an experience of remorse, and a request for renewal. The Bible illustrates this for us.

Repentance begins with the *admission of wrong*. Think of the Prodigal Son who, returning home to his father after blowing his inheritance on loose living, says, *"Father, I have sinned against heaven, and in your sight; I am no longer worthy to be called your son"* (Luke 15:18–19a). Or think of King David, who confessed to God after committing adultery and murder, *"Against you, you only, have I sinned and done what is evil in your sight"* (Psalm 51:4). These are personal admissions of guilt, but Old Testament prophets and priests also admitted the collective sins of God's people along with their own, as Nehemiah did: *"I and my father's house have sinned. We have acted very corruptly against You and have not kept the commandments, nor the statutes, nor the ordinances which You commanded Your servant Moses"* (Nehemiah 1:6–7 NASB).

Together with an admission of wrong, true repentance entails an *experience of remorse*. We don't just realize we're wrong and acknowledge it. We *grieve* our wrongdoing. We're sick about it. Remorse over our sin leads us to a healthy, godly sorrow (2 Corinthians 7:10), not to shame and guilt. The psalmist described his experience of remorse like this: *"My strength fails because of my iniquity, and my bones waste away"* (Psalm 31:10). Sin was felt as a strength-sapping, sorrowful, wasting heaviness (Psalm 32:3–4) that was impossible to ignore.

Finally, true repentance inspires a *request for renewal*. We don't want more of the same where our sin is concerned. We long to be changed from within, to be made new. *"Create in me a clean heart, O God,"* King David prayed when convicted of his sin, *"and renew a steadfast spirit within me"* (Psalm 51:10). When the Jews' national disobedience led to the destruction of Jerusalem, the prophet Jeremiah prayed, *"Restore us to You, O LORD, that we may be restored; renew our days as of old"* (Lamentations 5:21). One of the thieves crucified with Jesus not only acknowledged his wrongdoing, but as he faced death, he asked Jesus to make him new: *"Jesus, remember me when You come in Your kingdom!"* (Luke 23:42 NASB). True repentance begs for resulting change and the fruit that follows.

Let's look at two stories from Scripture and see if we can recognize genuine repentance. (Sometimes it's easier if the life we're looking at is not our own!)

COUNTERFEIT REPENTANCE

The first story is of Israel's first king, Saul.

God delivered his people after four hundred years of slavery in Egypt, protected and provided for them through forty years of wilderness wandering, and led them by prophets and judges for four hundred years. Their relationship with God as his people was unique—but they preferred what the pagan nations surrounding them had. God was their king, but that wasn't enough for them. They wanted a human king. Eventually, God gave them what they asked for. King Saul looked great on paper, but he was a disaster as a leader. Even though he had some military success, Saul was deeply flawed, and his pride and self-protection eventually became his downfall.

When God sent Saul into battle with the neighboring Amalekites, he ordered Saul to utterly destroy them, putting to death every man, woman, child, and animal. This is a challenging passage. We struggle to believe that God would command such a thing. How could a God of love and mercy require the death of an entire people? Our struggle helps us to see that we don't view sin as God does, which in turn means that we don't value his mercy as we should. God was just in his command. The Amalekites had profaned God and posed a spiritual and physical threat to Israel's survival. *"Utterly destroy all that he has,"*

God commanded, *"and do not spare him"* (1 Samuel 15:3 NASB). Well, Saul did defeat the Amalekites, but he did not completely destroy them, their king, or their livestock. He questioned the wisdom of God's judgment and substituted his own instead. (Don't be quick to judge Saul—we do this too—we're checkered with the unbelief that what God commands is true and good.)

Then to make matters worse, Saul lied to God's prophet Samuel about his failure to obey God's command. Before Samuel could say a word to Saul, Saul launched into his campaign of denial: *"Blessed be you to the LORD. I have performed the commandment of the LORD"* (1 Samuel 15:13). Except he hadn't. And Samuel knew he hadn't as he heard the bleating and lowing sounds of the Amalekites' very-much-alive sheep and oxen!

My teenage kids have a phrase that somehow seems appropriate here. "Really, now? Did you *really?*" Samuel may well have been thinking just that, but his response to Saul's blatant lie was a little more to the point. *"What then is this bleating of the sheep in my ears and the lowing of the oxen that I hear?"* (1 Samuel 15:14).

Instead of coming clean and owning his sin and deception, Saul doubled down. He blamed "the people" for sparing the Amalekite king and their choicest livestock, saying it was their decision, not his. And if that weren't enough, he then justified it by telling Samuel they did it to offer God a better sacrifice!

Saul denied his sin, blamed others instead of owning it, then tried to spiritualize it by saying it was for God's sake that he disobeyed!

Rightly, Samuel dropped the hammer on King Saul:

Has the LORD as great delight in burnt offerings and sacrifices,
as in obeying the voice of the LORD?
Behold, to obey is better than sacrifice,
and to listen than the fat of rams.
For rebellion is as the sin of divination,
and presumption is as iniquity and idolatry.
Because you have rejected the word of the LORD,
he has also rejected you from being king.
(1 Samuel 15:22–23)

When Saul saw Samuel's anger and realized the LORD was rejecting him because of his sin, Saul began to get it ... kind of. He said words of repentance, but his heart was not in them and his motives were not pure. *"I have transgressed,"* he admits to Samuel, *"now therefore please pardon my sin and return with me, that I may worship the LORD"* (1 Samuel 15:24). Saul wanted Samuel to accompany him in worship so that he could be seen as righteous before all the people, but his heart had not changed. He was not sorry he sinned. He was sorry he got caught. He was sorry that his sin could cause him to lose the throne and lose face.

Samuel followed Saul back to the people of Israel, and Saul worshiped the LORD before them; Samuel then called for Agag, king of the Amalekites, and in obedience to God's original command, hacked him to pieces with a sword. Then Saul and Samuel parted ways, never to meet again, and we're told that *"Samuel grieved over Saul. And the LORD regretted that he had made Saul king over Israel"* (1 Samuel 15:35).

So, what do you think? True repentance? Did Saul make an honest admission of wrong? Did he have a personal experience of remorse? Did he make a sincere request to God for renewal? No? Then in spite of his words of contrition and acts of public worship, there was no repentance.

GENUINE REPENTANCE

In contrast, consider Israel's *second* king, David, who also had occasion to repent.

David, too, disobeyed God and sinned—he was a man as deeply in need of grace as Saul or you or me. Like Saul, he wrestled with pride and self-protection. In fact, David got so full of himself that he committed adultery with another man's wife and arranged to have her husband murdered!

As with Saul, David had a truth-teller in his life: the prophet Nathan. Just as Samuel confronted Saul with his sin, Nathan confronted King David—but Nathan's method was more subtle. Instead of accusing David directly, Nathan told him a story sure to touch a former shepherd's heart: a story of a rich man with many flocks and herds who stole the only ewe of a poor man, a lamb his children treated as a household pet. David was incensed by the story and demanded that Nathan bring him the rich shepherd who stole another man's lamb so that he could be put to death. *"You are the man,"* Nathan said to David. And the truth floored David (2 Samuel 12:1–15).

Now here's where the stories of these two kings begin to diverge. Confronted with his sin, Saul stood his ground, denied his guilt, insisted on his own obedience, and blamed others. But David refused to stand on any ground but the mercy of God.

We know exactly what was going on in David's heart, because we have a record of his personal prayer of repentance in Psalm 51. He admitted his wrong-doing: *"According to the greatness of Your compassion blot out my transgressions. Wash me thoroughly from my iniquity and cleanse me from my sin. For I know my transgressions, and my sin is ever before me"* (Psalm 51:2–3 NASB). David called the transgression his, not someone else's. He called his sin, sin. He owned it.

David's remorse is clear. He was stained by his sin and broken with sorrow over it. *"Purify me with hyssop,"* he begged, *"and I shall be clean; wash me, and I shall be whiter than snow"* (Psalm 51:7). His sorrow ached like a physical wound: *"Let the bones which You have broken rejoice"* (v. 8 NASB).

Saul regretted his sin for its unfortunate consequences. David felt remorse over his sin because it hurt God. Remorse leads us to self-examination, and what we discover in our heart sends us running to God for forgiveness and rescue. *"Hide Your face from my sins,"* David pleaded with God, *"and blot out all my iniquities"* (v. 9 NASB).

You see, just confessing our sin is not repentance. Repentance is genuine when we turn from our sin and ask God to renew us. David did this: *"Create in me a clean heart, O God,"* he asked, *"and renew a steadfast spirit within me"* (v. 10 NASB). In other words, "Change me, O God, that I might not sin against you again. Renew my heart and produce the fruit in me that accompanies repentance."

This is genuine repentance. David's repentance doesn't just look spiritual—he's not just saying the right words and making a show of worship. He was deeply convicted, and his heart was changed. He moved toward God again, not away.

MOVED TO REPENTANCE

What draws someone's heart to repentance? What caused David to move toward God in the wake of his sin and Saul to move away? What fuels that? Paul told us in Romans 2:4 that it's God's kindness that leads us to repentance. The kindness of God compels us to repent. We presume upon his grace far too often, but when we understand his kindness—particularly his kindness to us demonstrated through the cross of Jesus—we're motivated to turn from our sin and run toward his grace (Romans 5:8).

God has delivered us from the kingdom of darkness into his marvelous light. He has called us sons and daughters of the King when we were slaves to sin. We deserve the same judgment that the Amalekites received, but instead, we have experienced the mercy of God. The more we remember this, the more we meditate upon the great grace extended to us through the cross of Christ, the more we become a people who see our sin, call it sin, confess it, and turn from it.

If you are not repenting of sin regularly, are you recalling the cross and remembering the kindness of God? Because it's his kindness that leads us time and time again to repentance (2 Timothy 2:24–26).

GROWING IN REPENTANCE

Let me add one more thing we sometimes forget. Repentance is not a "one and done." We don't repent once for our sins and never again. Repentance becomes a lifestyle as we grow in Christ. You might think that sanctification—the faithful work of God making us more and more like Jesus over our lifetime—would make repentance unnecessary. But that's just not true. As the Spirit continues to reveal God's holiness to us, our awareness of sin becomes sharper and more fine-tuned.

The chart on the following page helped me see this more clearly and illustrate it for others.[7]

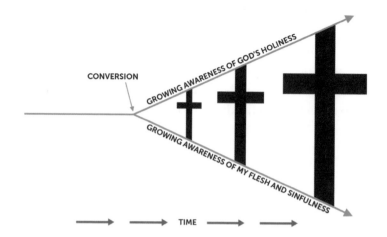

Imagine everything above the timeline represents our awareness of God's holiness and grandeur and perfection. Everything below it represents our awareness of our sin and our lack of holiness. The split in the line signifies our conversion. When God first saved us, he barely opened our eyes, if you will, to see both his holiness and our own sin. (We couldn't handle more than this dim view at first.) The gap between those two realities or lines is spanned in the drawing by the cross.

Graciously over time, God increases our awareness of his holiness and our sin. (As John Calvin has said, "Repentance is not merely the start of the Christian life, it is the Christian life."[8]) Consequently, the cross that spans the gap between his holiness and our sin appears larger as we grow in faith; and our understanding of Christ and his work on the cross for us becomes greater and more central to our daily lives. "Faith and repentance are not static," says Sinclair Ferguson, "they are lifelong realities of a new heart."[9]

We grow in repentance as we continue to consider God's great grace in light of our sin. By his grace I'm not struggling today with some of the same sins that I did when I was twenty; but he's opened my eyes to many less "visible" transgressions that I failed to recognize before. I'm seeing little crevices of sin in my heart that still require repentance, and God willing, when I'm sixty or eighty I will recognize my sin even more clearly than I do today.

When we fail to live as a people rooted in ongoing repentance, the cross of Jesus loses its majesty and the kindness of God loses its allure. Instead of resting in Christ's righteousness for us, we begin to trust in our own. When we trust in our own goodness or righteousness to make us right before God, we will either end up self-righteously prideful because we think we're actually pleasing God with our religious performance, or we'll be in despair as we see how utterly incapable we are of pleasing God in ourselves. Thus, the cross of Christ and his righteousness for us must be the foundation of our lives and the focus of our repentance.

If you and I are to become people of radical dependence we must be rooted in faithful prayer and genuine repentance. Together with you, I long for God to do what only he can do in and through us for his glory. Through his church, may we see souls saved, marriages healed, wayward prodigals returning home, addictions conquered, chains broken, relationships restored, families mended, abortions thwarted, racial healing realized, human trafficking abolished, the poor and needy served, widows and orphans brought in, and diseases healed! If those things and more are to happen, they will happen because we are a praying and repenting people, crying out like King David to our God: *"Against you, you only, have I sinned ... Create in me a clean heart, O God, and renew a right spirit within me"* (Psalm 51:4, 10).

QUESTIONS FOR REFLECTION

1. "The sin-and-denial cycle is a part of the human experience." Do you agree with this statement? Why or why not? Have you experienced this in your own life?

2. Why is repentance considered a key "root" in a lifestyle of radical dependence?

3. As you consider the "anatomy" needed for genuine repentance, which of these aspects has been most challenging for you in the past: an admission of wrong, an experience of remorse, or a request for renewal?

4. How is counterfeit repentance different from genuine repentance?

5. How does a growing awareness of your sinfulness lead to a growing awareness of God's holiness?

6. Is there an area in your life in which you are living in unrepentance? What are steps you need to take today or this week to embrace a lifestyle of dependence through repentance?

CHAPTER 7

ROOTED IN SELF-DENIAL AND SACRIFICE

AND HE SAID TO ALL, "IF ANYONE WOULD COME AFTER ME, LET HIM DENY HIMSELF AND TAKE UP HIS CROSS DAILY AND FOLLOW ME. FOR WHOEVER WOULD SAVE HIS LIFE WILL LOSE IT, BUT WHOEVER LOSES HIS LIFE FOR MY SAKE WILL SAVE IT. FOR WHAT DOES IT PROFIT A MAN IF HE GAINS THE WHOLE WORLD AND LOSES OR FORFEITS HIMSELF?"

(LUKE 9:23–25)

I like a pristine lawn. You know the kind I'm talking about: Vibrantly green. Well-manicured. Lush. Weed free. Now, rarely in my life have I *had* that sort of lawn … but I *do* like the idea of one. Whenever I walk past a well-manicured lawn, I always stop and admire it.

There's a good reason that in all my years of home ownership I've never had a perfectly pristine, flourishing lawn: they require a ton of really hard work. A visitor from "across the pond" once asked a groundskeeper at England's famed Eton College how its manicured lawns were kept so perfect. "It's simple," the good man replied. "Brush off the dew every morning, mow every other day, and roll them once a week."

"That's all?" the tourist asked.

"Absolutely," the expert said. "Do that for five hundred years, and you'll have a nice lawn too."

See what I mean about a lot of work?

DOWN FOR THE STRUGGLE

Anyone who wants a flourishing lawn in Atlanta, Georgia, is in for a battle. Because the things you *don't* want to grow in the soil of your lawn are going to spring up every day. Nutsedge, clover, dandelions, crabgrass ... do nothing, and those weeds are going to grow. On the other hand, the stuff you want to nurture and keep—the Bermuda grass, the zoysia grass, and fescue—those will need more thoughtful, hands-on tending and labor.

The Christian life is like that, too. The things we don't want to find growing in our hearts all too easily take root and thrive: selfishness, self-righteousness, arrogance, pride, materialism, envy, anger, lust ... these spring up without our lifting a finger, so to speak. If we want the good stuff to grow, we must get involved.

And there's a reason for this. Every single one of us has been born into sin according to the Scriptures. We are born with what I like to call the "Adamic residue" of an old, sinful nature, so that the things that come naturally to us are the very things that spiritually kill us. Unfortunately, those deadly things don't come with flashing red lights and warning bells. No, they do just the opposite. They promise us life. They pretend to offer us everything our souls long for.

But they lie.

That's the bad news. Here's the good news: those of us who are in Christ by faith—who have tasted his grace and experienced him as our rescuer and deliverer—have been given a new nature. The apostle Paul in 2 Corinthians 5:17 said it plainly, *"Therefore, if anyone is in Christ, he is a new creation. The old has passed away; behold, the new has come."* This new nature of the Spirit of God opposes our old nature. It helps us to desire new and different things, things that glorify God and orient us toward life the way he designed it to be. This new nature of life in Christ battles our old nature of sin and death, and our hearts and minds are the battleground (Romans 6).

Our old nature says, "Serve yourself, strive, rise to the top, do whatever you have to do to satisfy your own desires," and our culture often applauds this plan! But our new nature in Christ is oriented to a different agenda, a different goal.

Jesus described it like this: *"If anyone would come after me, let him deny himself and take up his cross daily and follow me. For whoever would save his life will lose it, but whoever loses his life for my sake will save it. For what does it profit a man if he gains the whole world and loses or forfeits himself?"* (Luke 9:23–25).

There it is, straight from the lips of Jesus. Our new nature, oriented toward the kingdom of God, demands a lifestyle of radical dependence on Jesus through *self-sacrifice and suffering.*

Everything about the kingdom of God that Jesus is calling us to is counter-cultural to the smaller kingdoms that beckon us. Which means that the Christian is called to a lifelong, daily battle.

Author Michael Green says, "Followers of Jesus must not forget that there is inevitably a lifelong battle to fight. They are called to follow their Master in suffering but are promised to share in his triumph. That note of spiritual struggle is often absent from the contemporary church, but it is a mark of authentic Christianity."[10]

THE CALL TO SELF-DENIAL AND SACRIFICE

Jesus was always clear about the root of self-denial and sacrifice he asked of his followers. He didn't say, "If anyone wishes to come after me, he might think about taking up his cross now and then and denying himself." He said, *"If anyone wishes to come after Me, he must deny himself, and take up his cross and follow Me"* (Mark 8:34 NASB). Self-denial and sacrifice weren't requirements buried somewhere in the fine print of the disciples' contract or hidden in the footnotes of a Jesus follower's guidebook. They were placed front and center by Jesus himself. Jesus not only spoke of self-denial and sacrifice, he embodied them.

But according to Mark's gospel his first disciples were no more eager to embrace self-denial and sacrifice than we are:

And he began to teach them that the Son of Man must suffer many things and be rejected by the elders and the chief priests and the scribes and be killed, and after three days rise again. And he said this plainly. And Peter took him aside and began to rebuke him. But turning and seeing his disciples, he rebuked Peter and said, "Get behind me, Satan! For you are not setting your mind on the things of God, but on the things of man."

And calling the crowd to him with his disciples, he said to them, "If anyone would come after me, let him deny himself and take up his cross and follow me. For whoever would save his life will lose it, but whoever loses his life for my sake and the gospel's will save it. For what does it profit a man to gain the

whole world and forfeit his soul? For what can a man give in return for his soul? For whoever is ashamed of me and of my words in this adulterous and sinful generation, of him will the Son of Man also be ashamed when he comes in the glory of his Father with the holy angels."
(Mark 8:31–38)

When he heard these words, Peter took Jesus aside and rebuked him. Self-denial and suffering were not what he—or the rest of the disciples—had in mind for their master, or for themselves. They were thinking of Jesus as a different kind of king, and of themselves as subjects of a different kind of kingdom. Peter heard Jesus say, "I have to die and be raised on the third day," and his gut response was, "Wait, no! Hold on. Aren't we going to challenge the rule of Rome? Restore the kingdom to Israel? Lead Israel to victory over her oppressors? What do you mean you have to die, Jesus?" They were confused about the true nature of the kingdom of God.

We are also easily confused. But as God's people—as his radically dependent followers—we need to remember three very important things. First, we are called to fight against confusion in our own hearts, confusion in the culture, and confusion in the church. Second, we are called to embrace and expect the suffering that accompanies following Christ as Savior and Messiah. And finally, we are called to understand the paradox that for the Christian, self-denial and suffering lead to flourishing of life and soul.

WE FIGHT AGAINST CONFUSION

There's no doubt Peter and the disciples had misunderstood the nature of the kingdom and God and the mission of the Son of God. They had misapplied years of prophetic scripture about the coming of the Messiah. When the Son of God arrived on the scene and did not act as they believed he would and should, they became confused and resistant. Their hearts did what the human heart so naturally does: construes and interprets the truth before us to fit our own desires; and what we desire most is almost always centered on our personal ease and comfort.

We are just as easily confused today. We're a people who still operate out of our old sin nature. Left untended, our selfishness and desire for ease and comfort grows like weeds in a yard until we decide, like Peter did, to shape the message of Jesus into something that will suit our own agenda, not his.

We must fight this confusion in our own hearts, in the world around us, and even in the church.

Modern culture—particularly our Western culture—indirectly and directly promotes self-satisfaction through messages that appeal to our self-interest. "You need [fill in the blank] to be complete." Or, "You'll never be satisfied without more [fill in the blank]." Or, "You're a good person who deserves plenty of [fill in the blank]."

We're offered countless goods and services every day designed to maximize our ease and comfort. Comfort and ease have become such pillars in our society that we have come to expect them as a given that every human should have. And the Church is not immune from those expectations either.

I'm sure you've heard health and wealth "gospel" messages that insist God never means for you to be sick, or poor, or in any way needy or dependent. Those who offer such messages may mean well, but they are sorely confused. God isn't primarily interested in our comfort and ease of life, and the aim of his kingdom is not temporal prosperity in the way of health and wealth. Though he might choose to sovereignly bless us with those things, he has something much bigger and better in mind for his followers.

WE EXPECT AND EMBRACE SUFFERING FOR CHRIST'S SAKE

Imagine yourself hearing Jesus' hard words along with Peter and the other disciples: *"If anyone wishes to come after Me, he must deny himself, and take up his cross and follow Me"* (Mark 8:34 NASB). Would you be fired up and ready to go, or thinking, "Wow. I'm not sure I'm cut out for *that*"? To follow Jesus is to be in conflict with ease and comfort. Dietrich Bonhoeffer, the Nazi resistor and German theologian, insisted that "When Christ calls a man, he bids him come and die."[11]

Christ followers should expect conflict, expect struggle, expect suffering. And not just expect these, but embrace them. Not because we're full of self-righteousness, enjoy suffering, or are weirdly proud of our pain, but because we follow a suffering Servant who has invited us into *his* kingdom rule and reign. He suffered. We will share in his sufferings.

The apostles Paul and Peter both spoke to this reality. Paul, in Philippians 3:10, wrote, *"That I may know him and the power of his resurrection, and may share his sufferings, becoming like him in his death."* And Peter wrote in 1 Peter 4:13: *"But rejoice insofar as you share Christ's sufferings, that you may also rejoice and be glad when his glory is revealed."*

You and I live in between the first and second coming of Christ. The kingdom of God for us is both now, and not yet. Jesus paid the price for our sin and defeated death by his own death and resurrection—but he has not yet returned to put Satan beneath his feet, once and for all, and usher in the fullness of his kingdom. He *will* come again to judge sin, satisfy justice, and wipe away every tear from our eyes (Revelation 21:4). But in the meantime, in a broken and fallen world, we cannot follow our King without counting the cost, and suffering is a part of that cost.

But we naturally resist the call to deny to ourselves and suffer in this life with Christ. We want a convenient Christianity. John Stott said it well when he wrote, "Large numbers of people have covered themselves with a decent, but thin, veneer of Christianity. They have allowed themselves to become a little bit involved; enough to be respectable, but not enough to be uncomfortable. Their religion is a great, soft cushion. It protects them from the hard unpleasantness of life, while changing its place and shape to suit their convenience."[12]

Church, let's not be a people in love with comfort and convenience. Let's be a people radically dependent upon our great God who we *know* is at work for his glory and our good, even in our self-denial and suffering. Maybe *especially* in them. As C.S. Lewis wrote in *The Problem of Pain*, "Pain insists upon being attended to. God whispers to us in our pleasures, speaks in our conscience, but shouts in our pain: it is his megaphone to rouse a deaf world."[13] It is in our God-ordained suffering that we become most keenly aware of his character.

WE KNOW SELF-DENIAL AND SUFFERING LEAD TO
FLOURISHING OF LIFE AND SOUL

Jesus' call to self-denial and sacrifice comes with the firm assurance that all who surrender their lives for his sake will find them and all who save their lives for their own sakes will lose them. That seems paradoxical, doesn't it? The more we lose our lives according to our own standards, the more we gain life according to his. *"For what does it profit a man,"* Jesus asked his followers, *"to gain the whole world and forfeit his soul?"* (Mark 8:36). I believe our Lord is calling us today to begin to identify and die to the ways in which we are trying to "gain the world."

When I was six years old a board game called Trivial Pursuit was a big deal. Our family played a version of the game called *Bible* Trivial Pursuit. My dad likes to tell a story about me that involves this game. I mean, he loves the story so much that he once submitted it to *Reader's Digest*, a popular magazine when I was a kid. I'm not sure I remember the event that well but I've heard the story so many times that it feels familiar. The Bible Trivial Pursuit game asked questions in categories, and when you answered a question correctly, you could fill up your wheel game piece with a pie-shaped wedge of plastic.

One night as we played the game, I got the category "Finish This Verse." The verse was, "What would it profit a man if he gained the whole word, and forfeited his _____?"

Man, it was on the tip of my tongue. I thought. And thought. And thought. I wanted to get it right, so I considered one word after another, until I finally landed on the one I was convinced was the right answer.

"What would it profit a man," I started, "if he gained the whole world and forfeited his … *own woman.*"

My parents fell out. I mean fell over and fell out. When they finally stopped laughing, my dad said, "Well it's not necessarily a bad answer there, buddy. I mean, it's not the *right* answer, but I understand what you're saying."

I may have gotten the answer wrong that night, but I still like the idea of filling in the blank. And I believe what we fill that blank with

---

says a lot about what we most value. What would it profit a man or woman if you gained the whole world and lost your job? Your home? Your spouse? Your children? Your reputation? Those are good things. But they're not *the* thing. Your soul is eternal. And self-denial and sacrifice of precious but not ultimate things *for the sake of following Jesus* will never disappoint us. Jesus Christ is the only One who gives us what our hearts were made to receive: himself.

We don't seek to be rooted in self-denial and sacrifice for the purpose of discipline, applause, or self-esteem. We value self-denial and sacrifice because Jesus said they lead to a bigger, more beautiful vision of life: a life that prizes Jesus more than anything else. A life where our souls are truly and finally satisfied in him and him alone.

WE PROCLAIM JESUS IS THE TREASURE

Matthew 13 tells the story of a man who discovered a treasure in a field and prized it so highly that *in his joy* he sold all he had to buy that field and keep its treasure. *In his joy* are the three most important words in this story. Do you know what the treasure of the kingdom of heaven is? It's not you or me or any good thing in this life. It's the joy-giving *King*. It's Jesus! He is the treasure. When we discover him—when our eyes are opened to his beauty—we see that he is the way, the truth, and the life. We get such a great vision of our life centered on him and his supremacy and glory and reign that we will find ourselves joyfully releasing other things to have more of him. Not self-denial, sacrifice and suffering for their own sake, but for the sake of having more of Jesus and being satisfied in him.

So, what are we to do? We're to proclaim that Jesus is the treasure and imitate the One who, *"for the joy set before Him endured the cross, despising the shame, and has sat down at the right hand of the throne of God"* (Hebrews 12:2 NASB). We're to deny ourselves and look to him—even in the suffering he calls us to—and discover life as he designed it to be.

QUESTIONS FOR REFLECTION

1. Why do you think suffering and self-denial are so counter-cultural? Do you think this is different from what the early church experienced? Why is it essential to living a lifestyle of radical dependence?

2. How did Jesus embody self-denial and sacrifice in his time on earth?

3. What confusion must we fight concerning the kingdom of God? What might this look like practically in your own life?

4. "Comfort and ease have become such pillars in our society that we have come to expect them as a given that every human should have." Have you known this to be true in your own life? If so, describe what it looks like.

5. How does believing Jesus to be our treasure give meaning to our lives in the midst of the suffering, self-denial, or sacrifice?

CHAPTER 8

ROOTED IN OBEDIENCE

"IF YOU LOVE ME, YOU WILL KEEP MY
COMMANDMENTS. AND I WILL ASK THE FATHER,
AND HE WILL GIVE YOU ANOTHER HELPER, TO
BE WITH YOU FOREVER, EVEN THE SPIRIT OF
TRUTH, WHOM THE WORLD CANNOT RECEIVE,
BECAUSE IT NEITHER SEES HIM NOR KNOWS
HIM. YOU KNOW HIM, FOR HE DWELLS WITH YOU
AND WILL BE IN YOU. I WILL NOT LEAVE YOU AS
ORPHANS; I WILL COME TO YOU. YET A LITTLE
WHILE AND THE WORLD WILL SEE ME NO MORE,
BUT YOU WILL SEE ME. BECAUSE I LIVE, YOU
ALSO WILL LIVE. IN THAT DAY YOU WILL KNOW
THAT I AM IN MY FATHER, AND YOU IN ME, AND
I IN YOU. WHOEVER HAS MY COMMANDMENTS
AND KEEPS THEM, HE IT IS WHO LOVES ME.
AND HE WHO LOVES ME WILL BE LOVED BY MY
FATHER, AND I WILL LOVE HIM AND MANIFEST
MYSELF TO HIM."

(JOHN 14:15-21)

Do you get all warm and fuzzy inside when you hear the word *duty?*
How about the word *obedience?*

Most of us, if we're honest, would say we carry a built-in resistance to the idea of following orders or obeying commands. When a thing becomes a "have to" or a "should," it begins to lose its appeal. Something in our human nature resists being told what to do, no matter how wise or well-meaning the instructions we receive might be.

One of my desires as a teacher of God's Word is to remove the stigma from the word *obey.* We can't go far into the Scriptures without encountering it, and Jesus certainly never shied away from talking about it. You and I can't avoid it either. If we're to be committed as individuals and as a church family to a lifestyle of radical dependence on God, I'm convinced *we must be rooted in obedience.*

WHICH IS IT, LAW OR GRACE? (YES)

Throughout its history, the Protestant church has been conflicted in its emphasis on obedience versus grace. For at least the last five hundred years, there have been great pendulum swings between rhythms of licentiousness and legalism in the church. It seems that we're either running hard from legalism and abusing grace or insisting on law-keeping and virtually ignoring grace. We can't seem to reconcile the two for long.

More recently, mainline Protestant denominations have struggled to emerge from a split that began almost one hundred years ago between churches that focused chiefly on the social implications of the gospel (feeding the hungry, caring for the marginalized, fighting for economic and social justice, etc.) and those that focused chiefly on gospel proclamation and preaching. The short of it was, more liberal Protestant churches began doing the good works of the church while increasingly losing their grip on the Scriptures and the gospel of grace. In response, more conservative churches increasingly doubled down on doctrinal truths and the preaching of the gospel while virtually ignoring gospel works, with its various social implications. To put it simply, the *demonstration* of the gospel became separated from its *proclamation,* and vice versa. What God desires to be "both/and" had become "either/or."

I've seen this struggle within my own denomination in various ways. I joined the Presbyterian Church in America (PCA) in 2005, having grown up in a different denomination. There is so much I love about the PCA, and I count it a joy and privilege to serve as a minister of the gospel in its ranks to this day. But fairly quickly upon joining the denomination, I observed something that concerned me. It seemed to me that in certain church cultures where the gospel of grace was championed—and wonderfully so—there developed such a fear of legalistic religious duty that people ran from biblical obedience. A devotion to obeying the commands of Christ out of a love for him was being too closely aligned with religious perfor   :e and, as a result, the grace of God was being abused.

A THIRD WAY

About the same time that I embraced the reformed doctrines of Presbyterianism, I began discovering some of Tim Keller's writings. (At that time, Keller was the pastor of Redeemer Presbyterian Church in New York City.) His take on the ways of religion (legalism) and irreligion (abuse of grace), beautifully illustrated in Jesus' parable of the prodigal son, was a revelation to me.

Keller argued that we are all prone to displace the authority of God in our lives and put ourselves in his place as judge, either by law keeping or law breaking: "There are two ways to be your own Savior and Lord," he writes. "One is by breaking all the moral laws and setting your own course, and one is by keeping all the moral laws and being very, very good."[14] The younger brother in Jesus' story chose the first way. The older brother chose the second. Both found themselves alienated from the heart of their father as a result. But there is a third way, says Keller. It's the way of the gospel of grace.

The gospel of Jesus Christ transforms our hearts and reorients our desires. It makes us new people. We are no longer destined to be non-conforming law breakers or conforming legalists. The grace of God through Jesus Christ births in us a new desire—weak and imperfect as it may be—to respond to God's love with willing, heartfelt obedience. The love shown to us in the gospel of grace makes us want to *live* the gospel in return!

I've observed this in my own heart and life. During my first three years on staff with Cru, I had experienced an inner struggle between the law and grace. I wanted to obey God because I wanted to be good. I tried to do everything right so that I might represent him well and point others to him. One day while reading through the gospel of John, the Holy Spirit began to connect the dots for me. John 14:15 jumped off the page: *"If you love me, you will keep my commandments."*

Then I read John 14:21: *"Whoever has my commandments and keeps them, he it is who loves me."*

For the first time, those words didn't feel condemning to me. They felt freeing. God's love and grace—not duty—is the fuel for my obedience to him.

A CHANGED HEART OBEYS

For a long time, I didn't think I loved Jesus much because my performance as a Christ follower was so far from perfect. I didn't understand back then that my love was purely a response to *his* (1 John 4:19 says we love because he first loved us!). The work God has done and is doing in me confirms his love for me and inspires my love for him. My heart is compelled to obey his commands because my heart has been, and is being, radically changed by his love. I can't tell you what a difference this made for me with regard to obedience.

Instead of striving all the time to do better and be better, I could enjoy the privilege and joy of responding to God's love by obeying him. I was beginning to see that the gospel of grace that had saved me did not leave me standing still. It was transforming my very heart and in turn, changing the motivation for everything I did. I wasn't saved by obeying God, I was obeying God joyfully and willingly because he saved me by his immeasurable grace.

The culmination of that season of reorientation was a shift from dutiful obligation to joyful obedience, and I have never been the same.

BEWARE OF OBEDIENCE TRAPS

There are three types of obedience traps, if you will, that I want to warn you about.

My own experience illustrates the first trap that believers fall into in this call to obedience: the performance trap. The **performance trap** is, in essence, the exhausting, life-stealing burden of trying to please God through religious performance and morality. As I illustrated in my story previously, the performance trap robs us of joy and roots our obedience in fear of God rather than love of God.

Having already focused a good amount on the performance trap, let's move on to the second one: the **thinking trap**. The practice of thinking deeply is a crucial Christian discipline. My use of "thinking trap" is not meant to disparage the importance of a Christian becoming more like Jesus in "the renewal of your mind" (Romans 12:2). It's simply a word picture I'm employing here to illustrate how often we can think we know better than God. In this trap, we think, consciously or subconsciously, that we know better than God what is right and just and good, so we rationalize our way around his commands.

We see examples of this thinking trap throughout Scripture. Jesus told the story of a master who entrusted his three servants with talents to invest in his absence. Two of the servants did as their master instructed, but the third thought better of his command. Instead of investing the talent he received, he buried it in the ground to ensure safekeeping. The servant explained his reasoning saying, *"Master, I knew you to be a hard man, reaping where you did not sow, and gathering where you scattered no seed, so I was afraid, and I went and hid your talent in the ground. Here, you have what is yours"* (Matthew 25:24–25). But the master was not pleased. He took the one buried talent and gave it to the servant who had invested as he was instructed, leaving the "thinking man" with nothing but a rebuke.

Jesus' interaction with a rich young ruler is another example. This bright, successful young man who had done many things right approached Jesus and asked him what he should do to "inherit eternal life." Jesus told him he already knew the commandments: *"Do not commit adultery. Do not murder, Do not steal, Do not bear false witness, Honor your father and mother"* (Luke 18:20). The rich young ruler was pleased to report he had done all these. *"One thing you still lack,"* Jesus replied. *"Sell all that you have and distribute to the poor, and you will have treasure in heaven; and come, follow me"* (v. 22).

The young man thought about it. And he decided against Jesus' command. It seemed like a bridge too far. A sacrifice too great. Maybe eternal life wasn't what he wanted, after all. And the Bible says he went away sad, for he was very, very rich.

As crazy as it sounds, we sometimes struggle with obedience because we think we know better than God what is good for us.

A fellow pastor on our staff, Caleb Click, tells a great story about his old beater of a Honda Accord that illustrates the thinking trap well. The car had survived a lot, according to Caleb, getting him through college, seminary, and several years of youth ministry. But for some reason Caleb got it in his head that oil changes in a car were not a necessity, but a scam perpetrated by dealers and mechanics to bleed money from naïve car owners. So, he ignored the sticker on his windshield, ignored the Honda owner's manual, and eventually ignored the red warning lights that appeared on his dashboard with increasing frequency. Until one day, driving down Washington Road in Augusta, Georgia, Caleb's trusty Honda had finally had enough.

He says he coasted to the side of the road with a sick feeling and began to wonder if he had been right about the oil change thing. I mean, he thought he knew better. He *thought* he was saving money. He *thought* he probably knew more about the inner workings of a Honda Accord than the designers of said machine. Turns out he didn't.

You and I are like the servant, the rich young ruler, and the now wiser young minister. We hear the commands of God but do not obey them, because we think we know better than he does. We don't. His wisdom and his ways are always for our good.

The last trap I want to warn you about is the trap of a **lagging heart.** Sometimes we know what obedience looks like. We love God and we know we should want to obey him. But we don't. At least not yet. Our heart says, "Yeah, I know, I know. But I'm just not feeling it. I don't want to obey God in this situation, even though I wish I did." What then? Well, when this happens it is time to train ourselves in willful obedience—doing what God commands and believing that our heart will catch up to the truth we know.

Sometimes my heart lags behind my head. Does yours? I know I should work out, because when I'm finished I'll feel better, and because it's just generally good for my health. But I don't always want to. In those nine out of ten instances, I have to train myself to choose the right thing and trust that in time my heart will want what's best for me. The more I do this, the more I begin to love the rhythm of obedience and the more my desire catches up.

I'd love it if I could obey God every time with a heart full of gratitude and desire. I want that. But experience tells me that won't always be the case. I've mentored a lot of young men over the years who struggle with an addiction to pornography. One time, a guy I was meeting with for accountability told me that when his desire overwhelmed him he figured he might as well act on the temptation because his heart was already full of lust and therefore, he was already guilty of the sin.

"Do you ever do anything with 100 percent pure motives?" I asked him.

He said no, he probably didn't. I told him I probably didn't either. But we talked it through and he decided in the end that it was better to obey with lesser motives than to disobey altogether. You would never say, "I'm mad enough to kill that person, so I might as well do it anyway," right? You might not feel loving, you might not feel like forgiving, but you would choose to obey even if you'd rather do just the opposite. That's training in righteousness. That's giving your lagging heart time to catch up with what you know God desires. The more we train our heart to love obedience, the more it eventually will.

DON'T LOVE OBEDIENCE. LOVE JESUS.

Obedience for the sake of obedience is not our ultimate goal. Obedience driven by fear of what God might do (if we don't obey) is not biblical obedience. Biblical obedience is driven by what God has already done on our behalf. The end result we're after is not to love obedience and grow in compliance; it's to love Jesus and grow in Christlikeness. The aim is not to fall more and more in love with the blessings of obedience, but to fall more and more in love with Jesus. This is exactly what Jesus was getting at when he said, *"If you love me, you will keep my commandments"* (John 14:15).

And why wouldn't we?

We who were once far off have been brought near by the blood of Christ.

We who were once condemned by our sin are now beloved in the righteousness of Christ.

We who were once enemies of God, deserving his wrath, are now children of God receiving his mercy.

We who were dead in the trespasses of our sins in which we once walked have been made alive with Christ.

By the grace and loving-kindness of our God, we have been redeemed.

Redeemed to walk in newness of life!

QUESTIONS FOR REFLECTION

1. What feelings or thoughts come to your mind and heart when you hear the words *duty* and *obedience*? How did this teaching challenge your preconceived notions?

2. Describe the biblical relationship between grace and law. Was there a time in your life in which you saw these concepts as being in opposition with one another?

3. "A changed heart obeys." How does this type of obedience bring delight in obeying rather than drudgery? How does this idea change the motivation for our obedience?

4. When we consider the three obedience traps (performance trap, thinking trap, and lagging heart), is there one in particular with which you have struggled? How does this teaching on obedience change your approach if you encounter this struggle in the future?

5. "The aim is not to fall more and more in love with the blessings of obedience, but to fall more and more in love with Jesus." How does the idea of being redeemed by Jesus spur us on to greater obedience to Jesus? What practical steps could you take in order to foster a deeper relationship with Jesus?

CHAPTER 9

ROOTED IN DISCIPLESHIP

AND JESUS CAME AND SAID TO THEM, "ALL AUTHORITY IN HEAVEN AND ON EARTH HAS BEEN GIVEN TO ME. GO THEREFORE AND MAKE DISCIPLES OF ALL NATIONS, BAPTIZING THEM IN THE NAME OF THE FATHER AND OF THE SON AND OF THE HOLY SPIRIT, TEACHING THEM TO OBSERVE ALL THAT I HAVE COMMANDED YOU. AND BEHOLD, I AM WITH YOU ALWAYS, TO THE END OF THE AGE."

(MATTHEW 28:18–20)

Not long after I became senior pastor at Perimeter, I engaged in a series of large and small-group gatherings focused on what it means for us to be a church rooted in radical dependence. These meetings were a time for me to share our leadership's vision for Perimeter's future, but they were also a great time to listen as our members related their personal experiences of our church.

One question I asked at each gathering (and a question I continue to ask our members one-on-one) is this: *What is it that you love about Perimeter Church?* I wanted to hear what our members are grateful for and what things inspire them to continue to invest in what God is doing in and through the church.

I heard a variety of different answers—wonderful stories of personal growth and transformation—but the answer I heard repeated most often was this: *discipleship.*

It was thrilling to hear men and women describe how life-on-life discipleship (either one-on-one or in small groups) had deepened their understanding of what it means to walk with God and opened up avenues and opportunities for their faith in Christ to grow and multiply.

Discipleship has been a part of Perimeter's DNA from the very beginning. We're not a perfect church. Far from it. There are many, many things we can and will do better in the days ahead, by God's grace. But one thing we have done faithfully for over forty years is prioritize and practice what we call life-on-life missional discipleship.

WHY DISCIPLESHIP?

If you've been at Perimeter a long time, you may not realize how unique our culture of discipleship truly is. Many twenty-first century Western believers have come to think of "church" as what happens between four walls somewhere on a given Sunday. The scope of church has been reduced to a weekly event designed to deliver stirring corporate worship and a spot-on, thirty-minute sermon.

Please don't misunderstand.

I *love* corporate worship and the precious gift God has given his people in the Sabbath day. The preaching and teaching of God's Word with the gathered church is an indispensable aspect of the Christian life. Many Christians neglect the rythms of the Sabbath and coprorate worship to their own harm. Emphasizing the biblical imperative to make disciples of all nations does not lessen the importance of corporate worship. I am aligning with Jesus' parting instructions to his followers, who were the first church planters:

All authority in heaven and on earth has been given to me. Go therefore and make disciples of all nations, baptizing them in the name of the Father and of the Son and of the Holy Spirit, teaching them to observe all that I have commanded you. And behold, I am with you always, to the end of the age. (Matthew 28:18–20)

Jesus lived a perfect life, took our sins upon his shoulders, and bore the wrath of God on the cross. He surrendered his life and then rose from the dead, defeating the due penalty of sin, which is death. Following his resurrection, the Son of God walked the earth for forty days and appeared to over five hundred people. And after all that, what is the last thing he wanted his disciples to hear before he ascended into heaven? *Discipleship.* Be a people rooted in making disciples.

Jesus envisioned that the kingdom of God would advance through people like you and me—people convinced that we've received something so worthy and of such great value that we are compelled to impart it to others, one life at a time. Just like he did.

It humbles me to think that this is how God planned from the beginning to grow his kingdom. Two thousand years later, here we are, devoting ourselves to the same glorious endeavor the first disciples did.

WHAT DISCIPLESHIP LOOKS LIKE

Not long after Jesus left this parting instruction to his disciples, a man who had persecuted Christians and terrorized the early church experienced a dramatic conversion and became—outside of Jesus, of course—perhaps the greatest disciple-maker ever. His name was Paul. His final instructions, written from a Roman jail, were also about disciple making. To his young friend and pastor-in-training, Timothy, Paul wrote:

You then, my child, be strengthened by the grace that is in Christ Jesus, and what you have heard from me in the presence of many witnesses entrust to faithful men, who will be able to teach others also. Share in suffering as a good soldier of Christ Jesus.
(2 Timothy 2:1–3)

Paul gave Timothy a blueprint for disciple making in these two short sentences. Discipleship requires a grace that strengthens, it involves a truth to entrust, and it carries with it a measure of hardship to endure.

A Grace that Strengthens

Grace not only fuels obedience, but also strengthens us for the work of discipleship. Before we can begin to disciple others, Paul said, we must be *strengthened by grace.* The task before us as disciple makers will be impossible for us to complete apart from the grace available

---

to us in Christ Jesus. We might be able to go a little while in our own strength, but eventually we'll be overcome by frustration, discouragement, disappointment, and fatigue, because making disciples for Christ requires Christ's power. We need a grace that strengthens us in order to do the work.

When you and I trust in Jesus as our Lord and Savior, he unites himself to us. We are in Christ and he is in us. This union connects us to all that Christ is and all that he possesses, including his strength. So, when Paul told Timothy to be strengthened by the grace that is in Christ Jesus, he encouraged his young friend to remember the grace that saved him. He reminded Timothy that without that grace he was hopeless and helpless, prone by birth to reject God and run from him. He wanted Timothy to remember his once-fatal condition and revel in God's great overture of grace that brought him from death to life.

His advice to his beloved friend is to keep on drawing from the storehouse of glorious, immeasurable grace he received when he first believed—to remember and ponder it daily. Because when we are faithful to remember God's saving grace in our lives, we are sustained and strengthened by that very grace.

I love how pastor Tony Merida says it. He says, "Our strength is not in how long we have been Christians, in how much we know about the Bible, or in how long we have been in ministry. Our strength, this very moment, is in the grace that is in Christ Jesus. Our strength is derived from our union with Jesus and is supercharged by our daily communication with Jesus."[15]

Discipleship flourishes best in the deep, strengthening bedrock of grace.

A Truth to Entrust

Strengthened by the grace in Christ Jesus, Paul instructed Timothy to take the truth passed on to him and entrust it to other faithful men. We have truth passed on to us too: the holy, God-breathed Word of God. It contains the gospel message and everything that is profitable for life and faith. We are not just to protect and preserve this truth, according to Paul. We are to entrust it to others who will do likewise.

The word *entrust* used here by Paul is the same word Jesus used on the cross when he prayed, *"Father, into your hands I commit [or entrust] my spirit!"* (Luke 23:46). Jesus was dying. Breathing his last. And he was saying to his Father, "All that I am, I'm entrusting into your hands, Father. All that is precious, my life, my spirit, my willing death, I'm placing in your hands." You and I are to entrust our lives and the precious truth of what it means to follow Jesus to faithful men and women, who will then do the same with others.

We'll make mistakes in the entrusting process. We won't do it perfectly. But that's part of the beauty of being disciple-makers: in our imperfect attempts to make disciples of Jesus, God gets all the glory as he uses crooked sticks to strike straight blows for the kingdom of God! As followers of Jesus we should be constantly on the watch for faithful men and women we can entrust with the truth of the gospel. And I'm not just talking about disseminating information. Discipleship is more than one follower of Christ teaching another follower a set of facts. It's one follower saying to another follower, "I'm running toward the One who is making me more like him. Would you run with me? Let's lock arms and run to Jesus together." We're committing to strengthen one another, hold each other accountable, and pick one another up when we're too tired to run ... journeying together, life-on-life, into the compassionate, strengthening, loving, merciful, renewing arms of Jesus.

A Hardship to Endure

Since we've already said that a life rooted in radical dependence on God will include self-denial and suffering, I'll only mention a few more things here as it applies to discipleship and hardship. Paul's call to Timothy to "share in suffering as a good soldier of Christ" shouldn't come as a surprise. I don't believe Paul was calling Timothy to share in his suffering, though. Sure, Paul's sufferings were well documented (2 Corinthians 11:16–28), and Timothy must have been a comfort to him in hard times, but I believe Paul was inviting Timothy to share in the way of Jesus' sufferings—the One Isaiah called the "man of sorrows" (Isaiah 53:3).

Jesus made disciples … and Jesus suffered. As his followers we can't avoid hardship. If we're obeying Jesus' command to make disciples, we're going to experience suffering, because *discipleship is costly.* It requires continually denying ourselves like he did.

In Philippians chapter 2, we're told that Jesus humbled himself, was made in the likeness of men, and became obedient unto death. He surrendered the riches of heaven to dwell among sinners and share in their weakness. He was opposed by the leaders of his own religion, mocked and betrayed, then abandoned by those closest to him in his last hours. Jesus knew loneliness and pain. He wept. He bled. He died.

The hardship he suffered was great, but so was the reward. When we devote ourselves to making disciples in the way of our Lord, we also understand that with it will come hardship in this life.

Not only is discipleship costly, *it's messy too.* The process of making disciples rarely works the way we expect it to. Have you noticed? I've idealized discipleship at times, and maybe you have too. I've imagined that I will live life with a group of faithful men and skillfully impart my wisdom to them … that we'll have the most enlightening Bible discussions you could ever imagine, that we'll fearlessly share our faith, and that everyone we speak to will fall to their knees and repent! In my naïve imagination discipleship is a neat, efficient, and always thrilling process. And it might be … except it's a people job. And people are messy and unpredictable. (I know because I am one.)

A very successful entrepreneur I know once told me that in his experience, 60 percent of his corporate ventures failed and only 40 percent succeeded. I immediately thought of my discipleship efforts and felt a little better. Even strengthened by the grace of God and entrusting the truth I've received to faithful people, my failures have far outnumbered my successes. It just doesn't always pan out the way I want it to.

Another reason it can feel messy and hard is because God calls you and me to entrust his truth to people who are like us, *and* very different from us. Many times, he's called me to invest in people whose challenges suck the life out of me, if I'm being honest. Perhaps it's because our personalities are very different, or our interests are different. Or maybe it's because our cultures are different and the work it takes to understand each other's contexts can be exhausting.

But isn't that the epitome of the gospel?! Let's be fair here … you and I sucked the very life out of Jesus. Literally! Yet, he pursued us anyway. The Son of God chases us down with a grace that won't quit. He's patient with us—long-suffering. And he gives us the strength and ability to be the same with others. People can be messy and inconvenient but that is never an excuse for not making disciples.

IT'S WORTH IT!

If you've ever been a part of a life-on-life discipling relationship with someone and you've seen the light come on, you know beyond a doubt that *it's worth it*. When the truth of the gospel begins to click, and you see another person experiencing the transforming power of a life in Christ, there's nothing like it. Nothing thrills me like hearing a fellow follower of Jesus say, "Jesus really is as amazing as you say he is! He's changing me in ways I never imagined! He is satisfying me at depths I've always longed for! I may be a mess in many ways, but the love and grace of Jesus is changing me day by day."

When you begin to see that happen, you become committed to the very thing God has called you to do. What a privilege it is to take the good news of the kingdom of God and entrust it to others who will then do the same!

Let me add one final word of encouragement here. Discipleship isn't for some elite group of Christians. It's for all of us … every believer.

Jesus didn't say, "Go therefore and make disciples of all nations, except those of you who aren't really people persons and don't have a lot of one-on-one charisma." He didn't say, "Go and make disciples only if you are a great communicator," or "Go and make disciples if you are doing everything 100 percent right in the Christian life, 100 percent of the time." He's ready and willing to work with what you've got. He provides the skill and strength through his Holy Spirit within you, so you don't have to be a "professional" Christian to pull this off.

The Enemy will try to convince you that you don't have what it takes to make disciples. Ignore him. What if the apostle Paul had bought those kinds of lies? Paul was less-than-impressive physically. He readily confessed his own less-than-stellar reviews to the Corinthians, "For some say, 'His letters are weighty and forceful, but in person he is unimpressive and his speaking amounts to nothing'" (2 Corinthians 10:10 NIV). Other literature of the time reported that Paul was small in size, balding, and bow-legged with bushy eyebrows and a long nose. Here's the point: Paul was not a particularly good speaker, nor did he have the kind of personality or appearance that drew people to him. What if he had allowed himself to become insecure to the point of not pursuing others towards discipleship? But instead he was strengthened by grace, entrusted with truth, and willing to endure hardship for the sake of Jesus Christ. And we are reaping the benefits of his ministry to this day.

So, here's the question for us: As believers who are radically dependent on God, will we be disciple makers as Jesus commanded? Will we build God's kingdom life-on-life, one man, one woman at a time? And if so, then who is the Paul to your Timothy, and the Timothy to your Paul? Who are the men and women who can lead you to a greater understanding of God's truth, and who do you know who is younger in the faith, that you, through a life-on-life expression of the gospel, can lead to a greater experience of the Christian life?

If you don't know where to start, let me make a suggestion. Don't wait for someone to approach you. Be brave. Be proactive. Discipleship is imparting the foundational truths of the Christian faith in a life-on-life context to help others grow into maturity in Christ. So, making disciples may begin with sharing your faith with an unbeliever. It could involve helping new believers grow in their faith. Or it could be more mature believers sharing life together in a way that encourages each to a deeper dependence on God. Let's take this model of life-on-life discipleship handed down to us from our predecessors and build upon it. As the spirit of grace empowers us, let's be a people radically dependent upon God to obey Jesus' command to make disciples, expanding his kingdom one life at a time.

QUESTIONS FOR REFLECTION

1. Has discipleship played a role in your own spiritual development? If so, take a moment to recall men and women who have invested in your life, thanking God for them.

2. How was discipleship an integral part of the early church and the expansion of the gospel?

3. Do you consider yourself as one with "a truth to entrust"? Are there things about your life or your past that keep you from being part of this mission of discipleship? How might God use our inadequacies and imperfections to showcase to others his gospel of grace?

4. How does the idea of discipleship being "messy" cause you fear? Relief? Do you believe that the goodness of God can be displayed in the messiness of your own life?

5. When you reflect on the things in which you often invest your time and resources, why is investing in the lives of others a more lasting and worthwhile endeavor?

CHAPTER 10

ROOTED IN FORGIVENESS AND GENEROSITY

THE LORD IS MERCIFUL AND GRACIOUS, SLOW TO ANGER AND ABOUNDING IN STEADFAST LOVE. HE WILL NOT ALWAYS CHIDE, NOR WILL HE KEEP HIS ANGER FOREVER. HE DOES NOT DEAL WITH US ACCORDING TO OUR SINS, NOR REPAY US ACCORDING TO OUR INIQUITIES.

(PSALM 103:8–10)

RADICAL FORGIVENESS

On June 17, 2015, a young white man named Dylann Roof walked into the Emanuel African Methodist Episcopal Church in Charleston, South Carolina. He was quickly invited by several church members to join them in Bible study. These members were black. He sat with them for forty-five minutes as they studied the Word of God together. Then, motivated by evil racist ideology, he did what he had planned to do from the moment he walked in. He pulled out a gun and began shooting, murdering nine people.

Roof later confessed that he chose Emanuel as his target because he knew that it would be a place where black people would be gathered. He then said that he identified as a white nationalist and that he was sure that the white race was superior to all others. I recount this difficult and enraging account just to say this: Dylann Roof would be very hard to forgive.

That's why the rest of the story is so amazing...

Two days later, the loved ones of those murdered by Roof gathered in a courtroom. Roof was there too. Well, kind of. He wasn't in the room in person, but rather on a two-way video screen being simulcast from another room in the courthouse, for his safety. No one knew how the family members of the victims might respond. So, with Dylann before them on a video screen, they looked directly into his eyes and did the unthinkable. *They forgave him.*

They'd had no time to heal. They hadn't even buried their dead. Their worlds were still spinning. Emotions were high. In the moment that most people would justifiably unleash their righteous anger upon the perpetrator of such personal pain ... they forgave. They demonstrated an other-worldly forgiveness that was instinctive to their character.

The first family member stood and spoke through tears: "I just want everybody to know, to you, I forgive you. You took something very precious away from me. I will never talk to her ever again. I will never be able to hold her again, but I forgive you. And have mercy on your soul. You hurt me, you hurt a lot of people, but God forgive you, and I forgive you."[16]

As soon as she had spoken, another family member stood and came forward to the microphone, saying, "I forgive you and my family forgives you but we would like you to take this opportunity to repent. Repent, confess, give your life to the one who matters the most, Christ, so he can change it, and change your ways no matter what happened to you and you'll be okay through that. And better off than how you are right now."[17]

Yet another victim's loved one came forward and said, "I'm a work in progress, and I acknowledge that I am very angry but one thing Depayne ... taught me [is that] we are the family that love built. We have no room for hate, so we have to forgive."[18]

And it kept on going from there as one after another came to the microphone and expressed what many might say would be inexpressible in a moment like that.

More recently a similar scene unfolded in a Dallas, Texas, courtroom when eighteen year-old Brandt Jean forgave the female police officer who shot and killed his brother Botham while he sat in his own living room eating ice cream. Jean told the convicted officer he loved her and that he didn't want her to go to jail. He bore no ill will toward her, he said. "If you truly are sorry—I know I can speak for myself—I forgive you," he said. "And I know if you go to God and ask him, he will forgive you."[19] Then he asked the judge for permission to approach and embrace the weeping officer. The judge granted his request and the two embraced as the courtroom watched—and cried—in awe of what had just taken place.

Reports of these remarkable encounters went viral within minutes, and it's easy to see why: they were both stunning examples of radical forgiveness. Either these people were crazy or they were filled with something—or *Someone*—so uncommonly unique that the world didn't know what to make of it. It's not *natural* to extend forgiveness to someone who has committed atrocities against your wife or mother, brother or sister, father or husband, or friend. I mean, *who does that?*

I want to pause here and admit that both of these stories of radical forgiveness have many underlying complexities. The forgiveness I'm describing is not the whole story. Racial tensions boiled over as a result of both stories, and those tensions still exist. Sadly, we saw the evil underbelly of racial injustice manifest itself again in various ways in 2020. There is much for the church to engage with and discuss on this matter. My heart is not to overlook these challenges or simplify them. For the sake of the focus of this chapter, my heart is simply to point to the critical nature of forgiveness displayed in each instance.

Regardless of our situations, what comes naturally to us *all* is not forgiveness, but revenge. We naturally demand "an eye for an eye and a tooth for a tooth." We cry out for justice to the God whose *"righteousness and justice are the foundation of his throne"* (Psalm 97:2). We're not by nature generous forgivers or givers. But what is modeled for us in Scripture is something completely different. In God's Word we see forgiveness demonstrated in shocking ways.

Consider two familiar stories with me—one from the New Testament and one from the Old—that help us see radical forgiveness received and extended in ways that inspired grace-filled generosity.

FORGIVENESS RECEIVED

Zacchaeus was a rich tax collector from Jericho. He was a well-off Jew hated by other Jews. His job was to collect taxes for Rome, effectively profiting off of the oppression of his fellow countrymen. To make matters worse he was a chief tax collector known to skim off the top of his take, pocketing some of what he collected for himself.

Luke's gospel tells us that Jesus entered Jericho and was passing through, and Zacchaeus was seeking to see who Jesus was. Maybe he'd heard stories of Jesus' teaching or miracles. Maybe he'd heard the rabbis in his town talking about the identity of this new teacher, wondering if he might be "the one." In any case, Zacchaeus wanted to see this Jesus for himself.

But there was one problem. Zacchaeus was "vertically challenged." The brother was short! So, to see Jesus over the crowds, he had to climb a tree. When Jesus spotted him, he told him to come down, and that he was going to be staying at Zacchaeus's house while he was in Jericho! (I love that Jesus invited himself over!) Can you imagine how stunned the crowd must have been that this Rabbi would want to spend time with someone as vile and deplorable as a tax collector? Zacchaeus received Jesus into his home, and apparently into his heart, too, for we learn from Zacchaeus's own lips that he became a changed man. The fruit was immediate: *"Behold, Lord, the half of my goods I give to the poor. And if I have defrauded anyone of anything, I restore it fourfold"* (Luke 19:8). Jesus confirmed this change: *"Today salvation has come to this house, since he also is a son of Abraham"* (v. 9).

Zacchaeus received Jesus into his home and called him "Lord." Then he described what Jesus' forgiveness compelled him to do—a change that hit him right in the pocketbook. He's gave half of all he owned to the poor. Straight up. And for anyone whom he defrauded (and the list was no doubt long!) he was going to restore what he took *times four*. Jewish law only required that one fifth of the debt be repaid, and other places required double. But Zacchaeus was so radically changed by Jesus' generous forgiveness that he went above and beyond. One who has been forgiven much, gives much—even over and above what the law requires.

I can imagine what others at the table that night must have thought: "This is crazy! This tax collector has lost his mind!" But Zacchaeus couldn't have cared less. People who have been radically forgiven through the person and power of Jesus Christ are people who forgive much and give much in Jesus' name.

FORGIVENESS EXTENDED

Another story that models radical forgiveness for us is the story of Joseph (Genesis 45, 46). Joseph was one of the twelve sons of Jacob. Old Jacob played favorites, and clearly Joseph was his. His brothers knew it and they hated Joseph for it. When Joseph told his brothers about a dream he'd had in which they all bowed down to him, they became so angry they wanted to kill him. Instead, they sold him into slavery and told their father he'd been killed by a wild animal! To say these brothers of Joseph were jealous and filled with hate would be an understatement.

Joseph ended up in Egypt, a slave in the house of Pharaoh (king of Egypt). Through many years of ups and downs he came to be a trusted advisor to Pharaoh, second in command in all of Egypt! Pharaoh gave Joseph free reign over his kingdom—so Joseph's long-ago dream of power really came to pass. In those previous dreams, God told Joseph of coming famines, so when they did come, he was prepared. Knowing there was food in Egypt while they were starving in Canaan, Joseph's brothers traveled to Pharaoh's court to seek aid. They didn't know it, but the very brother they sold into slavery was now the man in charge over all of Egypt! They no longer recognized him—he now looked like an Egyptian prince—but of course, Joseph recognized them.

What happened next between these hopelessly estranged brothers is remarkable. Powerful. Improbable. Radical.

First, Joseph revealed himself to them. Then he forgave them.

I am your brother, Joseph, whom you sold into Egypt. And now do not be distressed or angry with yourselves because you sold me here, for God sent me before you to preserve life. For the famine has been in the land these two years, and there are yet five years in which there will be neither plowing nor harvest. And God sent me before you to preserve for you a remnant on earth, and to keep alive for you many survivors.
(Genesis 45:4–7)

Isn't that what you would have done? No? Me either.

I might have been rubbing my palms together, thinking "Vengeance is mine!" But vengeance is *not* mine. Vengeance is the Lord's—and in his grace—mercy and forgiveness are mine.

But Joseph doesn't just let them off the hook. He doesn't say "No harm, no foul" and then dismiss them. He doesn't hand them off to an underling to feed, equip with supplies, and then ship back home for good. No. In fact he did the exact opposite.

His generosity is shocking. In essence he said, "I'm bringing you to live with me until this famine is over. I've saved the best land for you. You, your children, your children's children, your flocks, your herds and our father, Jacob are coming here. I'm going to care for you myself."

Joseph forgave his brothers, then in a stunning display of generosity, he gave them more than they ever imagined he might. He was lavish in his generosity because he was near to the heart of God—and God's heart toward those he loves is both forgiving and generous. Joseph's story is a foreshadowing of an even greater rescue story that was still yet to come. You know it. It's the story of Jesus.

He is the beloved Son sent by God, who suffered at the hands of evil men, took God's wrath upon himself, and established us forever in grace. We deserve God's punishment for our sins, but instead he pours it out on Jesus. And like Joseph with his brothers, Jesus draws us to himself, reconciles us with the Father, and gives us a place where we can dwell with him and flourish forever.

NEAR TO THE HEART OF GOD

Joseph extended radical forgiveness. So did the people of Emanuel AME Church in Charleston, and the brother of Botham Jean in Dallas. They did so, not out of their own nature or through their own sheer willpower, but by the grace and mercy of God. Forgiveness is naturally far, far from our hearts, but it's never been far from God's.

Throughout the Scriptures, from the Old Testament to the New, we see the heart of God laser-focused on mercy, grace, and forgiveness. David said in Psalm 103 that the Lord is merciful and gracious, slow to anger and abounding in steadfast love:

He does not deal with us according to our sins, nor repay us according to our iniquities. For as high as the heavens are above the earth, so great is his steadfast love toward those who fear him; as far as the east is from the west, so far does he remove our transgressions from us. As a father shows compassion to his children, so the LORD *shows compassion to those who fear him. For he knows our frame; he remembers that we are dust.*
(Psalm 103:10–14)

These words point to the Messiah who would shoulder the sins of the people and take upon himself God's just and righteous wrath. God was willing to pour out judgment *on his Son*—the only One who never deserved it—so that he might justly and mercifully pour out love and forgiveness on us.

The prophet Micah wondered at such forgiveness:

Who is a God like you, pardoning iniquity and passing over transgression for the remnant of his inheritance? He does not retain his anger forever, because he delights in steadfast love.
(Micah 7:18)

Who is a God like our God? There is none. The way God extends forgiveness to his people is radical and overwhelming. Those of us who follow Jesus and are being made into his image are called to be as radically forgiving and generous as he is. As people who are near to the heart of God, we are fueled to live the way Christ called us to live, by his power that dwells within us.

And we aren't to forgive and then dismiss others or forgive and barely tolerate them. That's not what Jesus did! He didn't say to us, "I'll forgive you and maybe you can become my lowest-of-the-low, provisional servants." No. His forgiveness made us sons and daughters of the living God! Can a people who have received so much fail to go before the Lord in radical dependence and ask, "God, how would you have me forgive and give as one who has been forgiven and given so much?" Through Christ, God has lavished his grace on us. He is a generous and forgiving Father. May he make us a generous and forgiving people—and may the glory be his forever.

QUESTIONS FOR REFLECTION

1. As you reflect on these stories of radical forgiveness, which one stands out to you most? Can you relate? Is there a situation, present or past, in which you have chosen forgiveness over revenge or hate?

2. How do instances of radical forgiveness preach the gospel message louder than simply spoken word?

3. How do the concepts of forgiveness and generosity relate to one another? How do you see both played out in Christ's work on the cross?

4. "Those of us who follow Jesus and are being made into his image are called to be as radically forgiving and generous as he is." In what way is this instruction daunting? How has God, through Jesus, given you everything you need to live out such forgiveness and generosity?

5. Is there someone in your life for whom you are harboring unforgiveness? Is there someone from whom you need to seek forgiveness?

CHAPTER 11

ROOTED IN
THANKSGIVING

AND LET THE PEACE OF CHRIST RULE IN YOUR HEARTS, TO WHICH INDEED YOU WERE CALLED IN ONE BODY. AND BE THANKFUL. LET THE WORD OF CHRIST DWELL IN YOU RICHLY, TEACHING AND ADMONISHING ONE ANOTHER IN ALL WISDOM, SINGING PSALMS AND HYMNS AND SPIRITUAL SONGS, WITH THANKFULNESS IN YOUR HEARTS TO GOD. AND WHATEVER YOU DO, IN WORD OR DEED, DO EVERYTHING IN THE NAME OF THE LORD JESUS, GIVING THANKS TO GOD THE FATHER THROUGH HIM.

(COLOSSIANS 3:15–17)

If I told you I had an inexpensive, over-the-counter remedy that would improve your overall physical and mental health, increase your resilience to trauma, and make you more productive, would you want to try it? I'm sure you would. I have great news, in my experience, thankfulness does all of these things!

So far in the book, we've looked into the root system required for a lifestyle of radical dependence upon God. We've said that to become a flourishing people and a flourishing church we must—individually and corporately—be radically rooted in prayer, repentance, self-denial and sacrifice, obedience, discipleship, and forgiveness and generosity. The last root we'll explore is thanksgiving.

In his book *Respectable Sins*, Jerry Bridges introduces a list of sins that Christians don't generally think of as "that serious." He places ingratitude among them. "We can readily identify sin in the immoral or unethical conduct of people in society at large," says Bridges. "But we often fail to see it in what I call the 'acceptable sins of the saints.' In effect, we, like society at large, live in denial of our sin."[20]

It's hard for us to imagine that something as seemingly benign as thanklessness is really a sin. But many times throughout scripture, we are exhorted to be a people who give thanks.

In Colossians 3:17 Paul said to *"do it all in the name of the Lord Jesus, giving thanks to God the Father"* (NIV), and in Ephesians 5:20 he exhorted believers to *"[give] thanks always and for everything to God the Father in the name of our Lord Jesus Christ."* To the church at Thessalonica he wrote *"Rejoice always, pray without ceasing, give thanks in all circumstances; for this is the will of God in Christ Jesus for you"* (1 Thessalonians 5:16–18).

These verses characterize thankfulness as one of the primary expressions of a heart that has been made new and is filled with the Spirit of God. Conversely, unthankfulness is an expression of a heart that is darkened and far from God (Romans 1:21).

But how in the world are we to live out such a high and seemingly impossible calling? Surely Paul didn't literally mean we were to be thankful "always and for everything," right? And could "in all circumstances" possibly mean "all"?

And if there's no wiggle room in those imperatives, can we possibly hope to be *that* thankful?

Well, no. We can't.

I hope you're not shocked.

I'm being realistic. We honestly can't. This kind of gratitude is a reality we will never achieve if we attempt to live it out in our own power and ability. Left to our own devices, we're more likely to think of all the ways we might be bitter or frustrated rather than being thankful. "Always and for everything" gratitude requires radical dependence upon God and his empowering Spirit within us. He must transform us from the inside out with a heart of thanksgiving. And I'm convinced that the transformation begins as we keep our focus on the love of God in his character and in his gospel.

OH GIVE THANKS TO THE LORD, FOR HE IS GOOD

Psalm 107, a psalm of David, beautifully carries us into the presence of God, helping us to see his character and the beautiful way that he loves us.

Look at how it begins:

Oh give thanks to the LORD, *for he is good, for his steadfast love endures forever! Let the redeemed of the* LORD *say so, whom he has redeemed from trouble.*
(Psalm 107:1–2)

As we've discussed, our circumstances on this side of heaven can be, and often are, incredibly painful and hard. There's no denying it. Each Tuesday morning our church staff prays together, and we pray over every single request we receive during the week from our church family. I see, and our staff sees, all that the Perimeter family is walking through: the hard diagnoses, the strained relationships, the troubled finances, the wayward children, the divorces, the deaths, the lost jobs, the anxiety and depression—we see it, and we pray for it. We beseech the Lord to intervene and heal and deliver and restore. But we also do something that you might not expect.

We thank God. We thank him for the truth that he is sovereignly reigning over all this and ordaining everything in our lives for our good and his glory. We thank him for the ways in which he is making his saints more like him through the troubles of this life. Most of all we thank him for his character and his steadfast love. These trials will not endure forever. But his love does. The harshness of the world and its trials does not begin to change the good, steadfast, loving character of God.

HE DELIVERS US

Through the rest of Psalm 107 the psalmist described the ways God delivers us. This song of praise was written *before* the coming of Christ, who is our Great Deliverer, but its words applied then and they apply to us even more today. Those of us who've known the saving mercy of Jesus can say along with David, "Yes! In Christ, God has delivered me from wandering, from affliction, from foolishness and fear. We can declare with the psalmist that he is ever steadfast in his love for me!"

The first thing we see is that God delivers the wanderer:

Some wandered in desert wastes, finding no way to a city to dwell in; hungry and thirsty, their soul fainted within them. Then they cried to the LORD *in their trouble, and he delivered them from their distress.*
(Psalm 107:4–6)

Can you relate? I can. Once I was wandering in dry, lifeless places. I was finding no good space to dwell. I was hungry and thirsty spiritually; my soul fainted within me—and it was only in God, through Jesus, that I began to find a satisfaction for my wandering heart.

God delivers the afflicted too:

Some sat in darkness and in the shadow of death, prisoners in affliction and in irons, for they had rebelled against the words of God, and spurned the counsel of the Most High. So he bowed their hearts down with hard labor; they fell down, with none to help. Then they cried to the LORD *in their trouble, and he delivered them from their distress. He brought them out of darkness and the shadow of death, and burst their bonds apart.*
(Psalm 107:10–14)

Have you known dark places? Places of affliction? Our God delivers us from those as well. We can cry out to him in trouble and distress—even in the shadow of death—and he can break the bonds of our affliction.

I'm especially grateful that God delivers us even from our own foolishness:

Some were fools through their sinful ways, and because of their iniquities suffered affliction; they loathed any kind of food, and they drew near to the gates of death. Then they cried to the LORD *in their trouble, and he delivered them from their distress. He sent out his word and healed them, and delivered them from their destruction.*
(Psalm 107:17–20)

Even when my troubles result from my own foolish actions or sinful ways, God still delivers me from my distress, and I thank him for his steadfast love!

Does fear plague you? Are you in a place that feels threatening or strange? Are storms—physical, emotional, or spiritual—looming near? Our God is greater than the elements, and the waters are never too rough or deep for him to navigate. He stills the storms, hushes the waves, and delivers us from the things that frighten us:

Some went down to the sea in ships, doing business on the great waters; they saw the deeds of the LORD, his wondrous works in the deep. For he commanded and raised the stormy wind, which lifted up the waves of the sea. They mounted up to heaven; they went down to the depths; their courage melted away in their evil plight; they reeled and staggered like drunken men and were at their wits' end. Then they cried to the LORD in their trouble, and he delivered them from their distress. He made the storm be still, and the waves of the sea were hushed. Then they were glad that the waters were quiet, and he brought them to their desired haven.
(Psalm 107:23–30)

How do we respond to such a good and wise and powerful deliverer? We give thanks! Let us thank the Lord for his steadfast love, for his wondrous works to the children of men!

Maybe every single one of these things are true of you right now. You're wandering, afflicted, foolish, and fearful. Thank him for his steadfast love. It never changes!

Maybe you're remembering a time when you were wandering, afflicted, foolish, or fearful, but not today. Thank him for delivering you from your distress. He's done it before. He can do it again. In his mercy God intervenes as our rescuer and deliverer. He may not change our circumstances, but he will certainly change our hearts, giving us the power, strength and perspective we need to go on. We can give thanks even in the midst of hard things because we know God's character and because we're the recipients of his grace.

A CITY TO LIVE IN

Giving thanks when circumstances are good is a very human thing to do. Giving thanks when circumstances are hard is a uniquely "Spirit of God" thing to do. Additionally, as the Spirit of God leads us, he also assures us of our future:

He turns a desert into pools of water, a parched land into springs of water. And there he lets the hungry dwell, and they establish a city to live in; they sow fields and plant vineyards and get a fruitful yield.
(Psalm 107:35–37)

There is so much to be thankful for in what God *will* do. Did you catch it? A city to live in. This psalm, though written long before Christ came the first time, is pointing us to what he will ultimately do when he comes again. Do you know how the Bible ends? What does the last chapter of Revelation describe? A city. Those of us who are in Christ will dwell in a beautiful city, the New Jerusalem, whose splendor and majesty we cannot begin to imagine. We will indeed be in a place where deserts have been turned into pools of water and parched land into springs; where we will not be hungry but will be filled up with the fullness of God.

Our place in this beautiful city is secured by the finished work of Jesus, the One who took God's wrath in our place, who arose and defeated death. We fix our eyes on him now, praising his character and the good news of his gospel, and say with the saints from every age, "Lord we thank you for your steadfast love!"

Father, change our hearts through the power of the Holy Spirit, and shape them to be more like your Son Jesus. Make us a grateful people giving thanks for who you are and all that you have done for us through your Son and our Savior, Jesus Christ. You are good, Father. We praise and thank you for your faithfulness, your kindness, your love, and your mercy. You are indeed our Great Deliverer. We want nothing more than to be a people radically dependent upon you—rooted in prayer, repentance, self-denial, sacrifice, obedience, discipleship, forgiveness, generosity, and thanksgiving. Do in and through us what only you can. And to you be the glory forever. Amen.

QUESTIONS FOR REFLECTION

1. Are you prone to gratitude? Does expressing thanks to God and to others come naturally to you?

2. Considering Bridges's inclusion of ingratitude as an "acceptable sin," do you agree with his assessment? What do you think are the greatest dangers of an ungrateful spirit?

3. Does God consider you inauthentic when you verbally give him thanks in seasons where your heart may not feel thankful? How do your words and songs of gratitude transform you into a more thankful person?

4. How is your faith bolstered by giving God thanks for the future work he will do, even when you don't know how, when, or what it may be?

5. As you reflect on the many roots of radical dependence—prayer, repentance, self-denial, sacrifice, obedience, discipleship, forgiveness, generosity, and thanksgiving—which of these might be the greatest challenge for you? Describe what it might look like to live radically dependent on God in that particular area.

BEING RADICALLY DEPENDENT IN A PANDEMIC

I ORIGINALLY COMPLETED THE FIRST MANUSCRIPT FOR THIS BOOK ONLY WEEKS BEFORE THE COVID-19 PANDEMIC HIT THE UNITED STATES IN EARLY MARCH OF 2020. WITH ITS ONSET, WE DECIDED TO HIT PAUSE ON THIS PROJECT SO THAT I COULD FOCUS ALL OF MY ENERGY ON LEADING PERIMETER CHURCH THROUGH THE MANY TRIALS AND DIFFICULTIES THAT 2020 BROUGHT.

Reflecting now, the Lord's timing is always everything, from humorous to mysterious to perfect. As I was preaching the sermon series that this book is adapted from in the fall of 2019, I declared several times to the congregation that the Lord was calling us to be radically dependent upon him in new and fresh ways. Little did I know what he had in store for 2020! To say that he led us into new and fresh ways to be radically dependent upon him would be a laughable understatement! From widespread health crisis to social and political unrest, the footing that many of us thought we had was suddenly crumbling beneath us as we found ourselves grasping for stability and normalcy. Though difficult, it's in seasons such as these that the Lord faithfully reveals our idols, rattles our allegiances, exposes our hidden agendas, illuminates our divisions, and disrupts our lives in such a way that causes us to realize that nothing we depend on outside of him will suffice. One of my favorite authors, Paul Tripp, has a term for this; he calls it God's "violent grace." Circumstances that we've been facing over the past year and half are indeed violent in their experience, but in a way that we may not always recognize, they are a measure of God's grace in that they are the very means by which we wake up from the doldrum of our lesser dependencies so that we may radically depend upon the maker, sustainer, and lover of our souls.

In the last chapter of this book, I highlighted the necessity and centrality of thanksgiving in the Christian life. God means it when he says that we are to be thankful in all things. On one hand, I certainly don't wish for the events and circumstance of 2020 to be repeated. But on the other hand, I'm grateful for them. Don't misunderstand me; I'm not grateful for the loss of life and the splintered friendships and broken families that resulted from the many expressions of sin and chaos that came with 2020. But I am grateful for the work that the Lord is doing in it and through it all. There is a pruning work that God is doing in his church. It's painful. But it's good. And it's teaching his people how to radically depend upon him and him alone. Most excitingly, in the hands of the Master Gardener this pruning will lead to more abundant fruit in the long run, for his glory.

Even a brief study of church history shows us that God often brings renewal and revival on the heels of crisis. Prayerfully and hopefully, he is preparing his church for a renewing work yet again in the months and years to come as he raises up a generation rooted in radical dependence upon him!

NOTES

1   John D. Witvliet, "Our Inestimable Privilege: Full, Conscious Participation in Worship," Calvin Institute of Christian Worship, June 1, 2004, https://worship.calvin.edu/resources/resource-library/our-inestimable-privilege-full-conscious-participation-in-worship/.

2   Ibid.

3   Oswald Chambers, *My Utmost for His Highest: The Key for the Greater Work* (Uhrichsville, OH: Barbour and Company, Inc, 1963), 291.

4   John Owen, "The Life, Thought, and Writings of John Owen," Quotes, 1616–83, https://johnowen.org/quotes/

5   Timothy Keller, *Prayer: Experiencing Awe and Intimacy with God* (New York, NY: Penguin Group, 2014), 5.

6   Paul Miller, *A Praying Life: Connecting with God in a Distracting World* (Colorado Springs, CO: NavPress, 2009), 125-126.

7   Paul Miller, *The Cross Chart.* In Eric Costa: "Am I Getting Worse?" Applying the Gospel, 2014, http://applyingthegospel.com/am-i-getting-worse/

8   Joel Beeke, "A Reformation of the Heart," TableTalk Magazine, 2017, https://tabletalkmagazine.com/posts/a-reformation-of-the-heart/

9   Sinclair B. Ferguson, *In Christ Alone: Living the Gospel Centered Life* (Lake Mary, FL: Reformation Trust, 2008), 158.

10   Michael Green, *The Bible Speaks Today: The Message of Matthew* (Nottingham, England: Inter-Varsity Press, 2000), 181.

11   Dietrich Bonhoeffer, *The Cost of Discipleship* (New York, NY: Touchstone, 1995), 89.

12   John Stott, *Basic Christianity* (Nottingham, England: Inter-Varsity Press, 2008), 140–141.

13   C.S. Lewis, *The Problem of Pain* (New York, NY: Macmillan Publishing Company, 1962), 93.

14   Timothy Keller, *The Prodigal God: Rediscovering the Heart of Christian Faith (New York, NY: Penguin Press,* 2008), 50-51.

15   Nadine Collier, "Charleston church shooting: What victims' families said to Dylann Roof," BBC News, June 19, 2015, https://www.bbc.com/news/world-us-canada-33185848

16   Anthony Thompson, Ibid.

17   Bethane Middleton-Brown, Ibid.

18   Brandt Jean, "Botham Jean's brother gave Amber Guyger a hug after the former cop was sentenced for his brother's murder in a powerful courtroom moment," Insider, October 2, 2019, https://www.insider.com/botham-jeans-brother-forgives-embraces-amber-guyger-2019-10

19   David Platt, Dr. Daniel Akin, & Tony Merida, *Christ-Centered Exposition: Exalting Jesus in 1 & 2 Timothy and Titus (Christ-Centered Exposition Commentary),* (Nashville, TN: B & H Publishing, 2013), 160.

20   Jerry Bridges, *Respectable Sins* (Colorado Springs, CO: NavPress, 2007), 16.